TRANSLATION

OF THE

SANHITÁ

OF

THE SÁMA VEDA

TRANSLATION

OF THE

SANHITÁ

OF

THE SÁMA VEDA.

BY

THE REV. J. STEVENSON, D.D.

GYAN

Published by

Gyan Publishing House
5, Ansari Road
Daryaganj, New Delhi-110002
Phone: 011-47034999, 9811692060
E-mail: books@gyanbooks.com

Distribution Network
gyanbooks.com
India, USA, Canada, UK, Australia

ISBN: 978-93-6280-366-5 (PB)
First Published, 1842

2nd Impression 2024

Printed at: Gyan Press, Delhi.

TRANSLATION OF THE SANHITÁ OF THE SÁMA VEDA
Author: J. STEVENSON

TRANSLATION

OF THE

SANHITÁ

OF

THE SÁMA VEDA.

BY

THE REV. J. STEVENSON, D.D.

LONDON:
PRINTED FOR THE ORIENTAL TRANSLATION FUND
OF GREAT BRITAIN AND IRELAND.
SOLD BY W. ALLEN AND CO., LEADENHALL STREET;
AND M. DUPRAT, PARIS.

M.DCCC.XLII.

THE TRANSLATOR'S PREFACE.

In introducing the Veda which is second in order, though first in excellence according to the Bhagavad-Gíta, to the notice of the English public, it seems proper that I should premise a few things relative to the matter and style of the original, and the helps used in making the translation.

SUBJECT OF THE SANHITÁ OF THE SÁMA VEDA.

The Sanhitá of the Sáma Veda consists of an arranged series of verses, directed to be sung especially at the Somayága or moon-plant sacrifice. The praises of the different deities who are supposed to honour the ceremony with their presence, and prayers for the prosperity of the worshippers and those connected with them, form the principal subject of these verses. Some of them are supposed to have the power of consecrating the fire into which the oblation is cast; and others, the Soma juice, of which it principally consists.

THE OBLATIONS OFFERED AT THE SOMAYÁGA.

The following particulars relative to the Somayága may be gathered from this Veda and its Commentary. When any one has determined to perform the moon-plant sacrifice, he invites Brahmans of the three principal classes,—Rig Vedi, Sáma Vedi, and Yajur Vedi Brahmans. The Atharva Vedi are not admissible, because, it is said, their profession being to destroy enemies, their presence would be inauspicious. The first thing to be done is to collect the moon-plant (sarcostema viminalis) and the araṅi-wood for kindling the sacred fire (premna spinosa); and this must be done in a moon-light night, and from the table-land on the top of a mountain. The moon-plants must be plucked up from the roots, not cut down, and after being stripped of their leaves, the bare stems are to be laid on a cart drawn by two rams or he-goats, and by them to be brought to the house of the Yajamána, the institutor of the sacrifice, for whose especial benefit and at whose expense all the ceremonies are performed. The stems of the plants are now deposited in the hall of oblation. Although the caul of the ram must form part of the oblation, I find nothing in the Veda about killing the animal, but I am told it is the practice to kill both of the rams. In the Abhangs of Tuka Ráma, a sage who flourished in the Deccan about three hundred years ago, the muzzling of the ram, and the beating of it to death by the fists of the Brahmans, are spoken of as necessary parts of this rite. His verses are to the following effect:

"'Beat to death the ram you've muzzled,
'And offer the Soma with sacred song;'
So they say, but yet I'm puzzled,
And half-suspect such worship wrong:
For rites like these are at best but scurvy,
That turn religion topsy-turvy."

Should the animal, during the above-mentioned operation,

utter the least sound, the omen is most inauspicious. I am told that after flaying the ram, and separating the caul, the flesh is cut into small pieces and cooked, being made into meat-balls with flour. One Brahman informant told me that they swallow these balls whole; another, that they simply apply them to the tip of their tongue. In the Matsya Purána eleven or thirteen kinds of flesh are ordered to be used at the feast to the manes of a Brahman's ancestors. In the Bháshya of this Veda, Kravyáda, 'eater of flesh,'[1] is conditionally used as the appellation of a holy Brahman; so that there is no innate improbability in the account I have given, though merely on hearsay authority. From the Bháshya it clearly appears that the Vaspá forms a part of the oblation to the gods.[2] It is explained by all the learned Brahmans I have met with as the caul or peritoneum, resembling, as they describe it, a piece of silk paper. All the refuse is collected in a bull's hide (go-twach), and buried at the conclusion of the ceremonies. This is done by express command, as recorded in the Rig Veda, I. Ashtaka, 1 Ádh. VII. Anuváka 5, 6.

The moon-plant stalks, when brought into the hall of oblation, are bruised by the Brahmans with stones, and then put between two planks of wood, that they may be thoroughly squeezed and the juice expressed. The stalks, with their expressed juice, are then placed over a strainer made of goats' hair, sprinkled with water, and squeezed by the fingers of the officiating Brahmans, one or two of which must be adorned with flat gold-rings. The juice, mixed with water, now makes its way through the

[1] Part I. Pr. I. 8. 8. [2] Part I. Pr. I. 6. 2.

strainer, and drops into the Drona Kalaśa, the receiving-vessel placed below, and situated at that part of the Yajnyavedi called the Yoni or womb,—a name, I conjecture, given sometimes to the vessel itself, though properly belonging to the place where it rests. The juice, already diluted with water, is in the Drona Kalaśa further mixed with barley, clarified butter, and the flour of a grain called by the Maráthas *wari*, the Sanscrit names of which are *nívára* and *trinadhánya*. It is now allowed to ferment till a spirit is formed, after which it is drawn off for oblations to the gods in a scoop called *śruch*, and in the ladle called *chamasa*, for consumption by the officiating Brahmans. The vessel, scoop, and ladle are all made of the wood of the catechu-tree (mimosa catechu). Nine days are mentioned in the Bháshya as required for the purificatory rites; but how many precede, and how many follow, I do not know. There are three oblations offered daily; one early in the morning, one at noon, and one at night. The Soma, when properly prepared, is a powerful spirit: it is said in this Veda to have intoxicated Śukra, the Guru of the Daityas,—to have made even Indra's face turn all awry while he was drinking it,—and, by its exhilarating principle, to have furnished him with that might, without which he could not have subdued the enemies of the gods.

OFFICIATING BRAHMANS.

The officiating Brahmans are distributed into six classes. There is, 1st, the Hotá, who chants the hymns of the Rig Veda; 2ndly, the Udgátá, who sings the verses of the Sáma; 3rdly, the Potá, who prepares the materials for oblation; 4thly, the Neshtá or Kartá, who pours the Soma, clarified butter, &c., into the sacred fire; 5thly, the Brahmá or Upadrishtá, who superintends and directs all the ceremonies; 6thly, the Rakshá, who with a Vajra or club of palás-wood, whose head is studded with spikes, stands at the door to ward off improper visitants. These, with the Yajamána or institutor of the sacrifice, form the seven classes of priests necessary at the Somayága.

THE SACRED FIRE.

The sacred fire ought always to be kept burning in a Brahman's house. The stricter sort accordingly always keep one fire burning, and some who are rich maintain three. The fire, kept alive by all rigid Brahmans, is called the Gárhapati or 'household guardian.' It is fed with the palás-wood (butea frondosa), and no other should be used. Twenty-one pieces, each a cubit long, are directed to be got ready against a sacrifice. At the commencement of the Somayága, fire is transferred from the Gárhapati to the Dakshina Agni or 'southern fire,' and to the Áhavaníya or 'oblation-receiving fire,' which is the most easterly of the three. Fire from heaven, obtained either from lightning or from the Sun, though by what process is not said, should also be added; and fire procured from the arańi-wood is to be joined to the other two: so that there are three different kinds of fire in each Kunda or fire-place. The process by which fire is obtained from wood is called churning, as it resembles that by which butter in India is separated from milk. The New Hollanders obtain fire from wood by a similar process. It consists in drilling one piece of arańi-wood into another by pulling a string tied to it with a jerk with the one hand, while the other is slackened, and so on alternately till the wood takes fire. The fire is received on cotton or flax held in the hand of an assistant Brahman.

THE HALL OF OBLATION.

The common Yajnyaśálá is a room in the inner part of a Brahman's house; it has a serpentine wall of between two and three feet high running through it, called the Yajnyavedi. This wall is divided into three parts, called the Saumika, Eshtika, and Páshtika. The floor is covered with the sacred Kuśa grass, with its roots cut, and regularly deposited for a carpeting. At the two ends of the Vedi, and in the centre, are the three Kundas or 'sacred fire-places.' The most easterly is square, the southern spherico-triangular, and the most westerly circular. These different Kundas are raised a little above the Vedi, and hollowed within to receive the fire. On great occasions like the Somayága a large shed is constructed in the court-yard or in the fields, and fitted up for a Yajnyaśálá.

YAJNYAVEDI.

THE AUSTERITIES THAT ACCOMPANY THE SINGING OF THE SÁMA VEDA.

The treatise called the Brahmana of the Sáma Veda is chiefly taken up in pointing out the austerities that must be practised before commencing and during the singing of this Veda. It is evidently from its style a modern work compared with the ancient hymns that form the Sanhitá, yet probably it is founded on ancient traditions. The first austerity mentioned is the Krichchhra Práyaśchitta, which requires for its performance twelve days. During the first three, the devotee eats only once, and that during the day; during the next three he eats once, but during the night; for the next three days he eats only provided that some one has given him food without his asking for it; and for the last three days he fasts entirely.

There is next the Atikrichchhra Práyaśchitta, corresponding to the above, only the penitent eats on no one day more than a single mouthful; and as if this were not a sufficient trial of Brahmanical endurance, there is next the Krichchhra Krichchhra, during nine days of which life is sustained by once drinking water, while on the three last even this simple beverage is denied. The singing of various sacred verses is to accompany these fasts. The first of these penances purifies, it is said, from common sins; the second, from deadly sins; and the third makes a man pure even as the gods. Such is the initiatory rite of this book of austerities, but it is a trifle to the concluding one, in the performance of which the devotee is commanded to live on milk during four months; then, having gone to the jungle, and having built for himself a shed, he is to enter it with his Kamandalu, or vessel for bathing, and fast twenty-one days without even drinking water. Should such voluntary abstinence be indeed possible, our physiologists will require to remodel their systems. Since the English occupation of the Marátha country, the Somayága has been three times performed within its boundaries; once at Násik, once at Puna, and once at Sáttara. The Brahmana declares that without austerities the sacred verses lose all their power; and since it is hardly to be supposed that privations like those above recorded were on these occasions submitted to, or are ever again likely to be endured, the votaries of Hinduism have a ready answer for those who ask why their sacred rites are not now attended with the effects ascribed to them in ancient times. As each of the penances mentioned in the Brahmana has a different object, it is probable that during the Somayága a selection may be made, and that the whole are not required.

CONCLUSION OF THE SOMAYÁGA.

The moon-plant sacrifice is not considered perfect unless there be a feast, and a distribution of presents to Brahmans at its conclusion. The viands of which the feast is composed are rice, sour curds mixed with barley-flour, cakes made with butter and sugar, along with potations of the moon-plant beverage. Cows, gold, horses, and provisions, are the principal gifts mentioned as necessary to be given to the officiating Brahmans.

THEOLOGY OF THIS VEDA.

The theology of this Veda differs considerably in detail from the modern systems of Hinduism, while yet its basis is the same. Soma, identified with the uncreated Spirit, holds the place of Brahma in the more modern Vedanta:

he is said to be Indra, Agni, and all the gods. All the gods perish, it is said, at the Great Pralaya; Soma alone remains, and becomes the originator of a new world. At the Pralaya it is said that the womb of Ocean contains all the gods. From these and similar expressions, however, nothing definite can be learned about the particular scheme of Hindu philosophy taught in the Vedas. Vishnu's Vámana Avatára is several times alluded to or mentioned, but none of the rest. Vishnu is but the younger brother of Indra, and inferior to him. Agni, the god of fire; Indra, the personified firmament; Mitra, the Sun; and Váyu, the wind, are the principal deities worshipped. After these come Vishnu; then the Sun, under the names Varuna, Púshá, Áditya, &c.; Varuna, as god of ocean; Yama, god of the infernal regions; the Aświni Kumáras, *i. e.* Beta and Gamma Arietis; the female divinities, Aditi, Saraswatí, Yamuná, *i. e.* the river Jumna, called Anśumatí; the waters generally; the wife and sisters of Agni; the Ribhu, deified Brahmans; the deified eagle Garuda; the genii of various sacrificial vessels and utensils; and the genius of sin. There is no mention of Brahmá, the creator, and none of Śiva, unless, as the author of the Bháshya is inclined to think, Śiva is but a form of Agni, to whom the name of Rudra is given in the Vedas. So greatly has the system of Hinduism been modified since these ancient hymns were composed, that the divinities adored as primary in them, have sunk down into a secondary rank; and others, inferior or unknown in those ancient times, have been raised to the place they once held.

THE METRE AND STYLE OF THE SÁMA VEDA.

The principal metres used in these hymns are the Gáyatri, Trishtup, and Jagati. The only peculiarity I have noticed is the introduction of the pluta or triple-time syllable; thus त्र३ stands as an iambus, whereas without this mark it would stand for a short syllable.[1]

The style of this Veda is very antiquated, compared with that of the Puránas and Sástras, and even of the Upanishads, though these last are called a part of the Vedas. The style of the Chhándogya Upanishad, though that work be said to belong to the Sáma Veda, is as different from that of the Sanhitá as the style of Chaucer is from that of Pope. In a word, a very slight inspection shows the two treatises to belong to quite different eras of the language. I have, while making this translation, collected above two thousand words, many of them of frequent occurrence, which are quite disguised by their uncommon inflexions, or not to be found even in Wilson's second edition of his Sanscrit Dictionary,—a very comprehensive digest, it will be admitted, of words current in the usual dialect of the language. These words, with the explanations of the commentator annexed, I have by me; and should an opportunity of publishing an edition of the original ever occur, they will furnish a useful accompaniment.

USE OF THE RIK IN THE SÁMA VEDA.

The Rig Veda is a collection of ancient hymns arranged according to their authors. The Sáma appears to

[1] See Part I. Pr. 1. 2. 8.

be a collection of verses arranged according to their subjects. I am of opinion that most of the verses, if not the whole, are taken from the Rik. The commentator for about two-thirds of the first Part mentions the author. I have searched in the Rik for all the verses ascribed to Madhuchhanda, Jetá, and Śunahśepha, and found the whole: the section of the Rik in which they are found I have noted in the margin. I feel persuaded that a similar search would have given the same result in regard to the others, as I have throughout the whole found verses I recognised as having seen in the Rig Veda.

MANUSCRIPTS OF THIS VEDA.

I have had before me two manuscripts of the Sanhitá, or text, in its proper combined form, and one of the Pada,—the text with the combined vowels resolved, and the ellipses supplied. I have also a copy in the Bháshya or commentary. All these different copies in the main agree very well. Such variations as materially affect the translation are noticed in their proper places. I have been indebted for the use of some of them to the Bombay branch of the Royal Asiatic Society, and for others to my friend Captain Shortreed, of the Trigonometrical Survey, without whose aid I could not at the first have obtained them.

HELPS USED IN MAKING THE TRANSLATION.

In making the translation I have followed throughout the commentary of Mádhava Áchárya, the famous Vidyáranya. He often appeals to Yáska, the author of the

Nirukti or 'Explanation of the difficult Words of the Vedas,' and I have occasionally consulted the same author, as well as the Nighanta, a vocabulary which contains many words not in common use except in the Vedas. Vidyáranya, it is well known, flourished at Vijayanagara in the fourteenth century of our era, during the reign of Bukka Raja. His brother, Sayana Ácharya, is the commentator on the Rig Veda.

AGE AND AUTHORS OF THE VEDAS.

It may be asked, what light do these hymns throw on the age and authors of the Veda? On the general subject of Hindu chronology they throw but little light, only the age of man is spoken of as being limited by about one hundred years. Comparatively, however, Yayáti and Turvaśa, who stand near the top of the list in the Soma dynasty, were ancients when some of the verses were written. Colebrooke's conclusion also as regards the authors is confirmed; for not only do we find the names of the Rishis prefixed to the texts, but in some instances introduced into the sacred Mantra itself. Viśwámitra, Vaśishtha, and the other names famous in Indian history then, were the authors of the Vedas. They lived before the time of Ráma Chandra; so that if Bentley's calculations approximate any thing near to the truth, we may say that some of the principal parts of these hymns were composed between one thousand and twelve hundred years before the Christian era.

In conclusion, I now resign my labours to the judgment of the candid, fully aware how much I need indulgence in reference to this translation. It is to be hoped that the facilities now afforded by the Oriental Translation Fund for bringing before the European public the treasures of Oriental literature will excite many to labour in this department. It is not till all the mysterious records of Hinduism have been brought to light, that we shall be able to take a comprehensive view of the Brahmanical system as a whole, and correct the mistakes which in a greater or less degree always attend limited information.

NOTE.—The absence of Dr. STEVENSON from England has deprived the following pages of the advantage of his final revision, and will account for such typographical mistakes as may occur, as well as for the occasional use of words or phrases which may be thought susceptible of correction or improvement. The manuscript being in general carefully transcribed, no plea has been left for misapprehension of the Translator's intention, and the transcript has been accordingly scrupulously followed: a very few obvious errors of the copyist have been corrected. Some few changes have also been made in the spelling of Hindu proper names, in order to preserve their consistency with forms already familiarly used.—H. H. W.

THE SÁMA VEDA.

PART I.

PRAPÁṪHAKA I.

FIRST DAŚATI.

Rich 1. *By Bharadwája Rishi.* Come, O Agni,[1] to the banquet of him who celebrates thy praise, to forward the offering. Herald[2] (of the gods), sit down on the sacred grass.

2. Thou, O Agni, hast been solemnly ordained by the gods to be inviter to all sacrifices performed in the world inhabited by men.

3. *By Medhátithi.* We invoke Agni, the messenger and herald of the gods, the possessor of all wealth,[3] that he may prosperously conduct our present sacrifice.

From Rig Veda, 1 Adh. 22 Varga, 1 Rich.

4. *By Bharadwája.* Agni has ever been the slaughterer of our foes. He is the possessor of

---

[1] Agni is the god of fire. [2] Hotá, the original word, means 'inviter or caller to the sacrifice.' [3] *Or* knowledge.

wealth;[1] he is celebrated in many various songs of praise; he is the shining and resplendent divinity, the object of our invocatory hymns.

5. *By Usaná.* O Agni, I praise thee our beloved guest,[2] dear to me as a friend; like a chariot (for celerity), and worthy of being considered the source of wisdom.[3]

6. *By Purumídha.* O Agni, save thou us, by thy mighty aids, from every foe, and from every man that hates us.[4]

7. *By Bharadwája.* O Agni, whether I now speak with true intonations or with false, I mean to praise thee. Come hither, therefore, and grow great by drinking this moon-plant juice.

8. *By Vatsa.* O Agni, I Vatsa, captivating thy mind, desire, by my song of praise, thy presence; therefore do thou come to me, even from the highest heavens.

9. *By Bharadwája.* O Agni, the Rishi Atharvan churned thee, in the beginning, from the lofty firmament, for the benefit of every offerer of sacrifice.

10. *By Vámadeva.* O Agni, destroyer of darkness, come to us for our effectual preservation, and to grant us an audience; for thou art a divine personage.

---

[1] *Or* desirer of sacrifice. [2] *Or* goer to sacrifices.

[3] *Or* wealth. [4] *Or, literally,* rid us *of* every foe, &c.

SECOND DAŚATI.

1. *By Ahi.* O divine Agni, these men praise thee, that they may obtain strength. Destroy their foes, together with their diseases.

2. *By Vámadeva.* I propitiate you[1] by my praises, who are the messenger of the gods, the possessor of all wealth, the presenter of the offering, the immortal, the great performer of sacrifice.

3. In thy immediate presence are ranged thy sacrifice-devouring, wealth-bestowing, offering-produced, everywhere-going sisters.[2]

4. *By Madhuchhanda.* O Agni, dispeller of dark- See Rig V. 1 Adh.
ness, day by day do we approach thee with en- 1 V. 1 R.
lightened minds, making our prostrations.

5. *By Śunahśepha, when ordered to praise Rudra.* Rig V. 2 Adh.
O (Agni), acquainted with the method of offering 24 V. 10 R.
up praise,[3] thou knowest[4] that kind of praise which procures the favour of Rudra, who carries on to perfection every sacrifice performed in the abodes of men.

6. *By Medhátithi.* Thou art invited to the ex- Rig V. 1 Adh.
cellent sacrifice, to drink the moon-plant juice; 36 V. 1 R.
therefore, O Agni, come attended by the Maruts.[5]

---

[1] The text has here the plural for the singular, which in this place I have followed. [2] Flames. [3] *Or* who by praises invites the gods. [4] *Or* do thou perform. [5] *i. e.* the winds.

Rig V. 2 Adh. 22 V. 1 R. 7. *By Śunahśepha.* I desire to worship thee, with religious rites, who art like a war-horse and blazest over the sacrifices.[1]

8. As Aurva and Bhrigu called on him, so do I call on the pure Agni, who resides in the ocean.[2]

9. Let the man who lights up Agni perform the ceremony[3] with an attentive mind. I am the man who lights up Agni with darkness-dispelling offerings.

10. *By Vatsa.* Now men gaze at the surpassing radiance, which in the days of old was united to the waters, and now shines forth in the firmament.

THIRD DAŚATI.

1. I long for thee, Agni, who growest super-eminently great amid sacrifices, that thou mayest strengthen our children.

2. *By Bharadwája.* Agni, by his fierce irradiations, restrains every cannibal foe. Agni gives us wealth equal to our desires.

3. *By Vámadeva.* O Agni, thou art great, and in motion all around; confer happiness on the people who desire to perform sacrifices to the gods.

---

[1] This and the three preceding verses will be found in the specified places of the Rig Veda. *Váravantam,* here rendered *war,* is there interpreted *long-tailed;* because, says the commentator, he drives away our foes, as a long-tailed horse drives away the flies. [2] *Or* the firmament. [3] *Or* receive instruction.

And come thou, and take thy seat on the sacred grass.[1]

4. *By Vaśishtha.* O divine Agni, preserve us from sin, and also from murder; and consume by thy burning flames every one who celebrates not thy praise.

5. *By Bharadwája.* O divine Agni, yoke thy horses, those excellent horses, that speedily convey thy chariot, and are manifested in all directions.

6. *By Vaśishtha.* O Agni, lord of the world, and the subject of our invocations, having laid hold of thee all-resplendent, and superemineently heroic, we place thee (in thy sacred recess).

7. *By Virúpa.* Agni, as the head of the heavenly hosts, stands pre-eminent, like the hump on a bull's neck. He, too, is lord of the earth, and refreshes us with the waters of the sky.

8. *By Śunahśepha.* Do thou, O Agni, mention among the gods this our gift, and repeat to them this our immortal hymn of praise. Rig V. 2 Adh. 22 V. 4 R.

9. *By Gopavana.* O Agni, maintainer of our bodily heat, the Rĭshi Gopavana first brought thee forth by his songs. Do thou, our purifier, listen to our invocations.

10. *By Vámadeva.* The lord of provisions, the

[1] The original is Varhi, and is the same as the famous Dharbha or Kus'a grass used at sacrifices, being spread on the floor instead of a mat, for the attendant Brahmans to sit on.

wise Agni, forwards the offerings to the gods, and confers rich rewards on the sacrificer.

11. *By Kańwa.* The vivifying rays draw forth, into the view of all, the divine Sun, the parent[1] of wealth.

Rig V. 1 Adh. 23 V. 7 R. 12. *By Medhátithi.* Praise Agni the wise, the divine, whose actions are guided by equity, who bestows gifts in lieu of sacrifice, and who is the destroyer of diseases.

13. *By Sindhudwípa and Ambarísha.* May the water-goddesses become to us sources of pleasure, in supplying us with water for ablutions; and of pleasure, by supplying us with water for drinking; and may they abundantly rain down happiness on us.

14. O lord of holy men, whose enlarged mind dost thou now fill with pleasure?—his, whose voice is employed in praising thee during this moon-plant sacrifice.

FOURTH DAŚATI.

1. *By Bharadwája.* We extol in every sacrifice, and in every song of praise, you, the powerful Agni, the immortal, the parent of wealth, and who is dear to us as a friend.

2. *By Bharga.* Save us, O Agni, by the first;[2] save us by the second;[3] save us, O lord of pro-

---

[1] *Or* parent of wisdom.

[2] The Rig Veda.

[3] The Yajur Veda.

visions, by the songs of the three; save us, O possessor of wealth, by those of the four (Vedas).

3. *By Trĭnpani.* O Agni, the source of manifold irradiations; O divinity encircled with unsullied splendour, as thou manifestedst thy glory in Bharadwája Rĭshi, so, O possessor of riches, our purifier, ever-young, do thou irradiate me.

4. *By Vaśishtha.* O Agni, who assumest the form of the sacred oblation, let the wise men be dear to thee, who invoke thee, and come laden with sacrificial goods, and divide among themselves the vast herds of cows[1] given by the host at sacrifices.[2]

5. *By Bharadwája.* O divine Agni, thou art the utterer of our praise, the sovereign of men, fiery in thy disposition, and ever watching the Rákshas. O lord of houses, thou art the mighty guardian of the heavens, and lovest the abodes of men.

6. *By Praskańwa.* O immortal Agni, origin of wealth, do thou, this morning, carry aloft thy variegated, darkness-dispelling treasures, for the benefit of the maker of the sacrifice, to the gods, who rise at the early dawn.

7. *By Trĭnpani.* O thou mine of wealth, thou art possessed of all various glories: along with protection, confer on us riches. Thou, O Agni, art

---

[1] Twelve hundred are reckoned in the Bháshya the portion of one Brahman! [2] These words are a paraphrase of *janánám*.

the forwarder to us of wealth; do thou also remember to give us deep cisterns of water for our sons.

8. *By Bharga.* O Agni, thou art truly great in every place; thou art the preserver, the faithful, the wise. O all-resplendent, all-bounteous; the learned Brahmans ever take up their abode close by thee.

9. *By Bharga.* O Agni, our purifier and our creator, liberally bestow on us, in reputable ways, food-increasing wealth, such as may make us honoured, such as is desired by many and is attended with the highest fame.

10. *By Saubhari.* The inviter of the gods, praised by all men, confers all the wealth any one possesses. The principal dishes of sweet liquid (moon-plant juice) are reserved for Agni; and let these eucharistic songs also be dedicated to the same divinity.

FIFTH DAŚATI.

1. *By Vaśishtha.* I invite, by this act of worship, Agni, the grandson of food,[1] the beloved, the omniscient, who repairs to (the sacrificial hall), the conductor of sacrifices to a fortunate issue, the herald appointed for the benefit of all the immortals.

2. *By Bharga.* Men cause thee to blaze forth

[1] The genealogy is thus reckoned in the Bháshya. Food makes the Brahman, and he the sacred fire.

for the benefit of their descendants, and to obtain those primeval waters from which the world has sprung. Thou, full of activity, bearest away the offering and the accompanying praises, and shinest among the gods.

3. *By Saubhari.* He, in whose hands the gods have placed all sacred rites, is eminently skilled in discerning the justness of sacred music; therefore let our voices spread abroad the praises of Agni, who has been produced in propitious circumstances, and exalts the institutor of sacrificial rites.

4. *By Manu.* During the sacred recitations, and while offering the oblations, I supplicate, in laudatory verses, to obtain special protection, Agni, the high-priest, the lifter up of the pestle, who sits on the sacred grass; and also the Maruts, Brahmańaspati, and the other gods.

5. *By Purumídha.* (O my soul,) do thou, in songs of praise, extol Agni, whose head is surrounded with glory,[1] that he may protect thee. O Purumídha, for the attaining of wealth and the procuring of excellent gifts for your family, extol the famous Agni, who assumes the human form.

6. Hear, O open-eared Agni, and ye sacrifice-receiving divinities that accompany him. Let Mitra and Aryama, along with all the gods who come to

---

[1] *Or* whose glory resides within, as digester and purifier.

our morning ceremonies, sit down on the sacred grass during the sacrifice.

7. *By Saubhari.* The divine Agni, brought down by Divodása, employs himself about mother Earth, with his mighty energy, after the manner of Indra,[1] and afterwards proceeds to the celestial mansions.

8. *By Medhátithi.* O possessor of all merit, do thou come from the earth, or from the lofty shining heavens, and obtaining increase in thy bodily proportions, by my songs, satisfy the desires of our children.

9. *By Viśwámitra.* O Agni, when worshipped, thou comest to the sacred wood and the maternal waters, nor dost thou suffer dissolution when thou disappearest to us, for thou art still present with us.

10. *By Praskańwa.* O Agni, Kańwa Manu first established thee, the possessor of radiance (in a sacred recess, as an object of worship,) to men for ever; then didst thou, oblation-born, all-expansive, whom men worship, display thy radiance.

SIXTH DAŚATI.

1. *By Vaśishtha.* The divine Agni, the conferrer of wealth, longs for your well-filled ladles; therefore pour them out (on the sacred fire) after you

---

[1] Either in educing the grain by his heat, or causing the rain to fall by means of lightning.

have filled them, in order that the god may prosper you.

2. *By Kañwa.* Let Brahmañaspati[1] come, let the sweet-voiced goddess come, to obtain the hero-producing, man-preserving sacrifice in which the peritoneum[2] is offered; and let the gods bear away for themselves our sacrifice.

3. *By Kañwa.* Stand up on high for our protection, like the divine Sun, (stand) on high to grant us food, when we call in sublime hymns and by our oblation-presenting priests.

4. *By Saubhari.* O possessor of riches, the man, who, to obtain wealth, takes thee from the sacred household recess, to place thee in the sacrificial recess, and gives thee offerings, he, O Agni, receives an heroic son, an adept in sacred song, and the supporter of thousands.

5. *By Kañwa.* We pray to thee, the lord paramount of the multitudes whose minds are intent on the performance of sacrifice. (We praise,) in laudatory hymns, that Agni whom our friends cause to shine forth (in all his splendour).

6. *By Trayukil.* This Agni has the conferring of vital power; he has the conferring of happiness, producing wealth, and of renowned descendants,

---

[1] *i. e.* Agni, as lord of food: the goddess afterwards mentioned is his wife. [2] Relative to the word 'peritoneum' see the Introduction.

and of herds of cows: he, too, has power to grant the destruction of our foes.

7. In our sacrifice thou art the householder, thou art the invoker of the gods, thou art the preparer of the oblation; thou art praised by all, and art possessed of inscrutable wisdom; thou servest the gods, and thou askest riches, to confer favours on us.

8.—*By Viśwámitra.* We, the men who are thy friends, beg of thee, all-resplendent, to grant us aid,—of thee, the grandson of the watery element,[1] possessed of all valuable kinds of riches, the performer of illustrious actions, the extirpator of our enemies, and void of wrath.[2]

SEVENTH DAŚATI.

1. *By Vámadeva.* Do ye serve with oblations, purify, and place with hymns of praise, in his recess at the altar of offering, the herald of the gods, and the sacrificer's household lord. Serve that Agni, who receives the offerings, and is worshipped by sacrifice; (serve) also the household gods.

2. *By Upastuta.* Truly wonderful is the method of acting exhibited by the recipient of praise, the ever-young; for he goes not to his mother to be suckled, but as soon as the breastless (wood) has

[1] Water nourishes wood, and from wood fire is churned out; hence the relationship according to the Bháshya.

[2] *Or* void of sin.

produced him, he instantly lays hold on the offering, and all at once arriving at manhood, performs his duty as messenger of the gods.

3. *By Vrĭhadukta.* (O Agni,) cause thy first and principal (lightning-produced) radiance, and thy second radiance (residing in the Sun), along with thy third (earth-born) radiance, to enter into their proper places in our sacred enclosure. Continue to be the all-resplendent, and the beloved of the gods; manifest thyself also in our sacrifice.[1]

4. *By Kutsa.* We forward this hymn of praise to thee, who art worthy of all worship, the parent of riches, with a mind as much on the alert as that of the charioteer who urges on his chariot. For, O Agni, thou art present in this our assembly, as the bestower of good things, and of a heart inclined to sing thy praise. May we never be guilty of extinguishing thee.

5. *By Bharadwája.* To be a head for themselves, the gods produced Agni, the indefatigable traveller from earth to heaven, who resides in all mankind, is brought forth in sacrifices, is the all-wise, the all-resplendent, the guest of the gods, our lord.

6. *By Bharadwája.* O Agni, the divine Brahmans obtain (wealth) from thee by their songs, as the

---

[1] *Or* in the excellent trees that produce thee.

winds (obtain) water from the ridges of the clouds. O recipient of praise, with our eucharistic voices do we come eagerly to thee, as war-horses rushing into the field of battle.

7. *By Vámadeva.* Secure the approbation of your own Agni, the lord of sacrifices,[1] the causer of grief,[2] the inviter of the gods, the faithful offerer of sacrifice for the two worlds, who existed before the clouds, yet without vitality, and who shines with golden radiance.

8. *By Vasishtha.* The radiant lord shines when praised; and his mouth, the receptacle of the offerings of clarified butter, is celebrated by the oblation-presenting sacrificers. This is that Agni who manifests his splendour at the natal place of the coruscations of the morning dawn.

9. *By Trisiras.* Agni traverses, by his own mighty power, the two worlds, and when he sends down rain he causes his mighty roarings to extend from the farthest to the nearest extremity of heaven; and, great in might, he grows greater still in the (ethereal) abode of waters.

10. *By Vasishtha.* O fellow-priests, bring forth by your manual labour from the sacred wood (Arañi) the everywhere-diffused Agni, who is borne

---

[1] *Or* who blazes over the sacrifice. [2] The original word is Rudra.

on the priests' hands (to his recess), who appears from afar, who is the protector of the sacrificer's family, and comes to his solemnities.

EIGHTH DAŚATI.

1. *By Budhagarishtí.* Agni is possessed of all wisdom, and comes with his brilliance to the sacrificers, like a milch-cow in the morning; and then his irradiations proceed aloft to the heavens, like the flocks of moving birds.

2. *By Vatsapríya.* The Brahmans lay hold on the mighty Agni, who subdues the earth, who is seized by the priests' fingers, who though in the company of fools is untainted by folly, the destroyer of the enemies' cities, and rendered propitious by praises, who is possessed of a most excellent understanding, has green mustachios, and a habitation of his own, and is worshipped with valuable productions.

3. *By Bharadwája.* Thou, O Agni, like the Sun, hast one lustre, which is white, and another which is red; thou art manifested in the two forms of day and night, and art expanded like the canopy of heaven. O possessor of food, thou preservest the understandings of all men. O nourishing Sun, grant that we may receive prosperity-causing presents in this sacrifice.[1]

---

[1] *Or* let the offering by which thou prosperest be here present.

4. *By Viśwámitra.* O Agni, grant to us, the performers of sacrifice, those supplies, by which many sacred rites can be performed, and cows which remain always profitable. O Agni, may we have sons and grandsons, the fathers of a numerous race, and may thy favourable regards be ever towards us.

5. *By Vatsapríya.* The herald of the gods, who is born in all the vigour of manhood, and who knows the heavens, goes to the dwellings of men, and also to the regions of the waters; he gives us riches, he lays hold of the moon-plants and other sacrificial viands, is the destroyer (of darkness), the possessor of wealth, and the protector of the body.

6. *By Vaśishṫha.* Agni delights in the priest of excellent qualities, who sings the praise of the shining, life-giving, illustrious god, who is possessed of a most merciful disposition towards man, and worthy of all praise, whose acts are like those of the mighty Indra.

7. *By Viśwámitra.* Agni, the producer of wealth, who is enclosed in the sacred wood, like a growing fœtus in a pregnant woman, is daily praised by watchful attendant priests.

8. *By Śaya.* O Agni, thou slewest the ancient Yátudhána giants, and the Rákshasas cannot conquer thee. Do thou slay the malicious fools that rise against us; but the eaters of flesh are not to be

liberated by thee,—they are reserved to be slain by the gods.[1]

NINTH DAŚATI.

1. *By Garga.* O Agni, to whose going no obstruction can be made, bring us strength-imparting provisions, lead us into the way of acquiring wealth and abundant supplies of food.

2. *By Vámadeva.* If a man lights up Agni,[2] and regularly presents him offerings, he becomes prosperous, and will enjoy happiness in a heavenly mansion.

3. *By Bharadwája.* Those large volumes of white expanding smoke go up to the heavens; and thou the purifier, when praised, shinest forth like the Sun, in all thy brightness.

4. *By Bharadwája.* Thou, O Agni, like a friend, conferrest fame, spreading wide as the world, on thy worshippers. O beholder of all things, as thou suppliest them with nourishment, so do thou supply us.

---

[1] *The flesh-eaters* may, according to my Brahmanical assistant, either be interpreted as meaning notorious sinners, such as Rávańa, who are reserved for the special vengeance of the gods; or holy Brahmans, who are not to be called away from the world by inferior ministers, but by the gods themselves. If the former be the sense, flesh-eaters means cannibals; if the latter, partakers of the sacrificial viands.

[2] *Or* the sacred fire.

5. *By Dwaita.* Agni, beloved by many, praised by mortals, in whose immortal fire all men cause the offering to blaze, is this morning our guest.

6. *By Vasuyava.* O thou, possessed of all various treasures, do thou greatly applaud the invocatory hymns addressed to Agni; for thee riches, thee provisions, ever attend, as the queen the king.

7. *By Gopavana.* By words, and hymns of praise, uttered with all my might, do I praise thee, Agni, the guest of every sacrificer, greatly beloved by the offerer of sacrificial viands, and who art present at the out-door sacrifice.[1]

8. *By Puru.* Provide abundance of food for the resplendent god Agni, whom, regarding as a friend, mortals place in the eastern receptacle, to celebrate his worship.

9. *By Gopavana.* We approach the foe-destroying, ancient, incarnate Agni, who shone forth most illustriously in the form of Śrutavana, the son of Arksha.

10. *By Vámadeva.* Agni, who is produced by the most excellent of all rites, is in an especial manner present, along with the other gods, in that same rite. He, too, is the father of Kaśyapa, the

---

[1] *Duryam:* the Bháshya on which is *yajnam; grihadwári bhavam.* Sacrifices at which multitudes attend are performed out of doors, in a temporary shed or pavilion erected for the purpose.

all-faithful, the mother of the human race,[1] the supreme lawgiver,[2] the all-wise.

TENTH DAŚATI.

1. *By Vámadeva.* We take refuge in King Soma, Varuńa, Agni, Áditya, Vishńu, Súrya, Brahmá, and Vrĭhaspati.

2. *By Vámadeva.* Those men who conquer the earth ascend to the lofty mansions of the sky from this nether world; even as the descendants of Angiras went up to heaven.

3. *By Vámadeva.* We light thee up, O Agni, that thou mayest confer on us great riches. Do thou therefore, O rainer of blessings, applaud our heaven-and-earth-produced, excellent, sacrificial viands.

4. *By Grĭtsamada.* What my soul utters, Agni lays to heart; he knows where sacrificial viands are served up. As the ring embraces the wheel, so does Agni all our eucharistic hymns.

5. *By Payu.* O Agni, by thy splendour destroy on every side the destructive splendour of our foes, and break down the might and prowess of the giant race of Yátudhána.

6. *By Praskańwa.* O Agni, prepare here an ex-

---

[1] As supplying them with rain, for their nourishment.

[2] In the original it is, the Manu.

cellent sacrifice for the Vasus, the Rudras, the Ádityas, and for the other gods, descendants of Manu, the givers of rain.

PRAPÁṬHAKA II.

FIRST DAŚATI.

1. *By Dírghatama.* O Agni, I offer to thee many oblations. I call on thee, lord of sacrifices: I am thine, as all in the house of a great man is his.

2. *By Viśwámitra.* Do ye satisfy the wise Agni, the herald of the gods, and holder up of light for the destruction of darkness, as of old, with many songs of praise.

3. *By Gautama.* O Agni, thou art lord of food and cows, and the offspring of Strength.[1] O thou parent of wealth, bestow on us stores of provisions.[2]

4. *By Viśwámitra.* O Agni, do thou, for the benefit of those who desire the divine favour, offer the oblation to the gods in this solemn sacrifice; for thou art conspicuous as the offerer of oblations, the inviter to the sacred rites, the recipient of praise, and the destroyer of murderous fiends.

5. *By Trita.* The seven mothers[3] entreat the

---

[1] The force used in churning the wood Arańi. [2] *Or* great fame. [3] *i. e.* the seven gods, seven offerings, or seven kinds of sacrifice.

wisdom of the sacrificers, for the prosperity of Agni, who is immoveable, and knows the place of riches.

6. *By Trimati.* May we rest daily under the influence of Agni's blessing, and may the wise Aditi[1] come to our protection; may she, the bestower of bliss, confer on us happiness, and destroy the murderers of our children.

7. *By Viśwamanas.* Praise the all-expanded sacrifice, to him who is the parent of wealth, distinguished by his wandering smoke, and possessed of irresistible radiance.

8. *By Viśwamanas.* The enemy cannot prevail against the wisdom of the man who gives to Agni, —the man who presents him with offerings.

9. *By Rĭgiswana.* O Agni, lord of holy men, remove far from us that repulsive, thievish, abominable foe, and make us the possessors of heaven.

10. *By Viśwamanas.* O heroic Agni, lord of men, through the hearing of my new song of praise, burn up, with thy fervid heat, the deceitful Rákshasas.

SECOND DAŚATI.

1. *By Saubhari.* O ye who come to utter praises, laud Agni, the bountiful giver, the bestower of

---

[1] Mother of the gods.

water,[1] the mighty, him who is encircled with shining radiance.

2. *By Saubhari.* O Agni, thou preservest thy friends by the production of food, and they are saved by thy aids and by heroic descendants.

3. *By Saubhari.* (O my soul), praise him whom, like the Sun, the gods have appointed to be the giver of gifts, and the fleet messenger, who presents the offerings to the gods.

4. *By Saubhari.* Let not Agni, the possessor of wealth, the recipient of many praises, the messenger and welcome inviter of the gods, and the prosperer of the sacrifice, be angry with us or our guests.

5. *By Saubhari.* O possessor of all valuable things, let Agni, appointed to be the inviter of the gods, be propitious to us, and let our offering be prosperous, our splendid sacrificial rites prosperous, and our hymns of praise prosperous.

6. *By Saubhari.* We pray to thee, the offerer of sacrifice, the bestower of gifts, the inviter of the gods, the immortal, that thou wouldest prosper this sacrifice.

7. *By Saubhari.* Bring such food, O Agni, as shall, in the sacrificial hall, subdue the cannibal Rákshasas, and the rage of malicious men.

8. *By Viśwamanas.* Agni, the lord of men, the

---

[1] *Or* accepter of sacrifice.

graceful, who is propitious to the descendant of a man, such as I am, will surely, without fail, slay all the Rákshasas.

[Here end the praises of Agni.]

THIRD DAŚATI.

1. *By Bharadwája.* While the moon-plant sacrifice is in progress, do thou, O my soul, in union with the other (chanters), sing the happiness of Indra, worshipped by multitudes, the bestower of gifts, with the eagerness with which the husbandman extols the happy condition of a powerful bull.

2. *By Śrutakaksha.* O Indra, performer of a hundred sacrifices, most resplendent (divinity), who rejoicest in the hymns of the celebrators of thy praise, do thou gladden them with a joy similar to thy own.

3. *By Haryata.* O my voice, do thou celebrate the cloud-shaped divinity, both whose ears are adorned with golden pendants; and the earth which furnishes water for our sacrifice.

4. *By Śrutakaksha.* O sons of Śrutakaksha, celebrate the praises of the gods, with all your soul, for the obtaining of horses; with all your soul, for the obtaining of cows; and with all your soul, to obtain a place in the heaven of Indra.

5. *By Śrutakaksha.* We present sacred viands to that Indra, who is the slaughterer of Vrĭtra.

May he, like a bull, become to us the rainer down of water.[1]

6. *By Devájámya.* O Indra, sender of rain, thou overcomest, by thy own internal strength, and by the aid of foreign powers, and by thy all-subduing patience: thou, too, art the rainer down of blessings.

7. *By Goshúkta and Súkti.* Our sacrifice magnifies Indra, who whirls round the earth,[2] and who causes thunder in the heavens.

8. *By Goshúkta and Súkti.* O Indra, as thou art lord of wealth, so may I become its sole monarch; and may the chanter at my solemnities become the possessor of herds of cows.

9. *By Medhátithi.* O performers of the moon-plant sacrifice, do ye, with all your might, advance the praise of the joyful Indra, and the moon-plant sacrifice of the all-prosperous hero.

10. *By Medhátithi.* O possessor of wealth, drink of this moon-plant juice, and eat to satisfaction of the sacrificial viands. O void of fear, we eat to please thee.

FOURTH DAŚATI.

1. *By Sukaksha.* O Sun, thou presentest thyself to Indra, famed for his riches, the sender down

---

[1] The Bháshya adds, yathá vrĭshabhah retasah varshitá, tadvad varshitá udakasya Sa bhavatu.

[2] *Or* changes the face of the ground.

of rain, the prosperer of the rites of men, the foe-destroyer.

2. *By Sukaksha.* O slayer of Vrĭtra, thou art the forwarder (to thy heavens) of whatever may be produced to-day (in our sacrifice); for, O Indra, all this world is under thy control.

3. *By Bharadwája.* That youthful Indra, who conducted far and near, under his secure guidance, Turvaśa and Yadu, is our friend.

4. *By Sukaksha.* O Indra, thou, who art the leader and conductor of great expeditions, let not our foes advance upon us, but grant that by thy aid we may gain the victory over them.

5. *By Madhuchhanda.* O Indra, bring for our protection wealth worthy of our acceptance, such that by its means we may completely conquer our foes, wealth ever enduring and ever increasing.

See Rig V. 1 Mandala. 3 Anuvak. 1 Sukta. 1 Rich.

6. *By Madhuchhanda.* In every great battle, and in every lesser conflict, we invoke the thunder-bolt-holding Indra to be our ally in contending with our foes.

Rig V. 1 M. 2 A. 4 S. 5 R.

7. *By Trĭśoka.* Indra drank the moon-plant juice of Kadru (the wife of Kaśyapa) in the full assembly, and there do ye magnify the might of Indra.

8. *By Vaśishtha.* O Indra, dispenser of rain, and possessor of wealth, we, the aspirants after thy favour, especially praise thee. Do thou acknowledge this our sacrifice.

9. *By Trĭśoka.* (Happy are) those who kindle up Agni, and at the same time spread the sacred grass, and of whom Indra, ever-young, is the friend.

10. *By Saśoka.* Cleave asunder all who hate us and oppress us, slay those who oppose us in war; and, O possessor of wealth, bring with thee the object of our desire.

FIFTH DAŚATI.

1. *By Kańwa.* Even here the smack of the whip they hold in their hands is heard, as well as the noise of their variegated chariots as they rattle along.

2. *By Trĭśoka.* O Indra, drinker of the moon-plant juice, these thy friends (the attendant priests) look on thee, with the affection that the cattle-feeder looks on his cattle.

3. *By Vatsa.* All the sacrificers employ themselves in appeasing Indra, and do homage to him as the rivers do to the sea.

4. *By Kusídina.* We entreat the gods, the senders down of rain, to render us their all-powerful protection for our preservation.

5. *By Medhátithi.* O (lord of food) Brahmańaspati, do thou for me, the chanter at the moon-plant banquet, as thou didst for Kakshívân, the son of Uśija.

6. *By Sukaksha.* Let the slayer of Vrĭtra convey

knowledge to my mind; and the possessor of many excellent qualities, the powerful Indra, hear me.

7. *By Sukaksha.* O divine Savitá,[1] provide for us abundant wealth, along with a numerous progeny; and keep the causer of death's fatal dream far from us.

8. *By Pragátha.* Wherever he who is the sender of rain, ever-young, all-embracing, unsubdued, takes up his abode, there the officiating priest performs his service.[2]

9. *By Vatsa.* In the region of the conglomerated clouds, and where the many waters meet, the wise Indra was produced by Intellect.

10. *By Irimiri.* Do ye praise with your voices (Indra), king of men, who is worthy of all praise, the subduer of heroes, and the bestower of gifts.

SIXTH DAŚATI.

1. *By Śrutakaksha.* Indra, whose features[3] have a divine gracefulness, has ever been in the habit of partaking of the strengthening sacrificial viands offered up by me, and of drinking the moon-plant juice, along with the barley-bree.

2. *By Medhátithi.* O possessor of immense riches, these our voices, ever uttering thy praises,

---

[1] The Sun, as the parent of natural productions. [2] *Or* even Brahmá, the Creator, serves thee. [3] The original means *nose*.

delight thee, as the voices of the milch-cows delight the herd of calves.

3. *By Gautama.* Doubtless, at the going down of the Sun, the rays of light reverently bend themselves towards the upper world, the region of the moon.[1]

4. *By Bharadwája.* Wherever Indra, the dispenser of copious showers of rain, goes, he brings along with him abundance of water, and in doing so he is joined by (the Sun in the character of) Púshá (the nourisher).

5. *By Yútadakshná.* The mother of the wealth-possessing, chariot-loving Maruts,[2] herself desirous of fame, and united to her sons, whom she brings forth from their residence, sends us down rain.

6. *By Sukaksha.* Come, O lord of the joy-inspiring juice, to our moon-plant banquet, along with thy horses named Harí. Come, with the horses Harí, to our moon-plant banquet.

7. *By Sukaksha.* Prepare pleasant offerings, such as magnify Indra, at this sacrifice. Get ready also the defect-atoning offering,[3] with all your might.

8. *By Vatsa.* I have embraced the wisdom derived from my truth-regarding father (Kańwa), and, like the Sun, I have become the beholder of all things.

---

[1] The Bh. adds, "and return to us in moonlight."

[2] Winds.

[3] *i. e.* the defects of *this sacrifice.*

9. *By Śunahśepha.* Let our praises, the procurers of wealth, and of stores of provisions, rest in the ever-joyful Indra; for we desire by means of these to obtain renown. Rig V. 1 M. 7 An. 7 S. 13 R.

10. *By Vámadeva.* Soma and Púshá both know all the blissful abodes, and they are appointed to convey to the gods the offering of the sacrificer and his wife.

SEVENTH DAŚATI.

1. *By Śrutakaksha.* Drink ye[1] of the prepared moon-plant juice, and extol Indra the all-subduing,[2] the performer of a hundred sacrifices,[3] and the bestower of gifts on men.

2. *By Vaśishtha.* Celebrate, my friends, the juice that inspires delight[4] into Indra, who drives the golden-coloured[5] horses, the drinker of the moon-plant juice.

3. *By Medhátithi.* We, the descendants of Kańwa, thy friends, the performers of sacrifice, anxious to worship thee, celebrate thee, O Indra, in sacred hymns.

---

[1] We have here *vah*, corresponding to the Latin *vos* in the nominative plural. [2] *Or* all-sustaining.

[3] *Hundred* alludes to the legend of the sacrifice of one hundred horses, by which the kingdom of heaven is obtained; or it means many.

[4] *Or* intoxicating, *maddening*; in the original, *mádanam*.

[5] *Or* green-coloured.

4. *By Śrutakaksha.* Let our voices praise the moon-plant juice offered to the joyful Indra, and let our sacrificing priests worship the god Soma.[1]

5. *By Irisni.* O Indra, this moon-plant juice has been purified for thee, and placed on the sacrificial grass: come quickly, and drink of it.

Rig V. 1 M. 2 An. 1 S. 1 R.

6. *By Madhuchhanda.* We call on thee, the performer of meritorious acts, day by day, as men call on the cow to the milking.

7. *By Śoka.* O dispenser of rain, I am preparing moon-plant juice for thee to drink in this moon-plant sacrifice. Partake of it, and enjoy the delight (it inspires).

8. *By Kuśidina.* O Indra, the moon-plant juice has been expressed for thee, in many spoons, and by many expressers. Drink of it, for thou art lord of all.

Rig V. 1 M. 7 An. 7 S. 7 R.

9. *By Śunahśepha.* O my friends, we call for protection, in every time of war,[2] on Indra, superior in might; on him we call in every engagement.[3]

Rig V. 1 M. 7 An. 7 S. 7 R.

10. *By Madhuchhanda.* O my friends, offerers of praise, sit down without delay, and sing to the honour of Indra.

---

[1] The moon-plant, or its juice, personified.

[2] *Or* in every offering.

[3] *Or* for every benefit.

EIGHTH DAŚATI.

1. *By Viśwámitra.* O lord of wealth, worthy of all praise, drink of this moon-plant juice, prepared by the might (inherent in the sacrificers).

2. *By Madhuchhanda.* Indra is celebrated as mighty from the times of old, therefore let might be ascribed to us by the holder of the thunderbolt; for his strength is equal to the heavens in greatness. Rig V. 1 M. 3 An. 1 S. 5 R.

3. *By Kuśidina.* O Indra, having laid hold of the vessel with thy mighty right hand, drink our renowned sparkling moon-plant juice, truly worthy of thy acceptance.

4. *By Priyamedhas.* I celebrate with my voice, as far as my knowledge permits, Indra, the lord of the moon-plant banquet, the son of truth,[1] the lord of holy men.

5. *By Vámadeva.* Let him, who is possessed of manifold excellences, who is always increasing, and our friend, be with us for our protection, by greatly forwarding the present sacrifice.

6. *By Śrutakaksha.* (O my soul), thou approachest, for thy protection, the ever-victorious Indra, extolled by the voices of all.

7. *By Medhátithi.* I beg wealth of Indra, the lord of the sacred assembly, the distinguished, the

---

[1] *Or* food.

beloved, the graceful, who remains near (the sacrificer).

8. *By Vámadeva.* Wherever, under the lofty heavens, thy goings may be, and in whatever paths like a fleet horse thou performest thy movements, there let our earth-born praises reach thy ear.

9. *By Sukaksha.* O Indra, performer of many meritorious acts,[1] bring to us stores of excellent meat and drink; for it is by this means that thou conferrest happiness on us.

10. *By Pútakaksha or Sukaksha.* Here is placed the juice of pressed moon-plants; let the Maruts drink of it, and let the twin sons of Aświni join in quaffing the royal beverage.

[End of the laudatory hymns addressed to various divinities.]

NINTH DAŚATI.

1. *By Devaja.* Our praises, moving towards Indra, go and reside in him, and beg of him superior might.

2. *By Godha.* O ye gods, we slaughter no victim, we use no sacrificial stake, we worship by the repetition of sacred verses.

3. *By Vámadeva.* I am now come, while the night is but departing. O offerer of praise, sing

---

[1] *Literally, as before,* "performer of a hundred sacrifices."

loudly and well. O thou, who walkest within the sacred enclosure, praise the (generative) god Sarita.

4. *By Praskańwa.* The matchless, lovely dawn has but just come to take up her abode in the heavens. I praise you, twin sons of Aświni, with all my might.

5. *By Gotama.* The invincible Indra slew ninety times nine of his foes with the bones obtained from the Rishi, Dadhícha's head.[1]

6. *By Madhuchhanda.* Come, O Indra, delight in our food, along with our preparations of moon-plant juice; for thou art the mighty one that excellest in strength. Rig V. 1 M. 1 A. 3 S. 2 R.

7. *By Vámadeva.* O Indra, slayer of our enemies, come to our sacred enclosure. O mighty god, come with all-prevailing aids.

8. *By Vatsa.* His might, whereby he encircles heaven and earth, as the skin does the body, appears in all its splendour.

9. *By Śunahśepha.* Thou approachest the sacrifice with the eagerness the male pigeon does his mate: let then these prayers of mine enter thine ear. Rig V. 1 M. 7 A. 7 S. 4 R.

10. *By Ullovatayana.* Let him come as our medicine, and the conferrer of happiness, and the

---

[1] This Rishi is said to have given up his life, that the bones of his head might be used to destroy the Asura Kálaśunja.

inspirer of vigour into our breasts; and let him prolong our lives.

TENTH DAŚATI.

1. *By Kańwa.* The man whom Varuna distinguishes for his knowledge, and Mitra and Aryamá protect, can never be slain by any one.

2. *By Vatsa.* Influenced by the desire of cows, of horses, and of chariots, we praise thee as aforetime; for thou art worthy to be praised by all offerers of sacrifice.

3. *By Vatsa.* These hymns of praise (are being sung) for thee, where they prepare the clarified butter and the mingled moon-plant juice.

4. *By Sukaksha.* In this sacred con-procuring ceremony, O subduer of hosts, and recipient of the praise of crowds of worshippers, we adore thee; for thou art present in every moon-plant sacrifice.

Rig V. 1 M. [illegible] A. 3 S. 10 R.

5. *By Madhuchhanda.* Let Saraswatí, who is our purifier, and by the sacrificial viands the supporter of strength, and the protectress of sacred rites, set her affections on our sacrifice.

6. *By Vámadeva.* Who is there that will satisfy Indra with the rites termed Nahúsha?[1] I will join such a one in offering the moon-plant juice to

---

[1] Otherwise called the Jyotishfoma.

the god: at the same time let Indra heap wealth upon us.

7. *By Irimi.* O Indra, come to the banquet of the sweet-flavoured expressed moon-plant juice, which is here set on the sacred grass in the midst of the holy assembly.

8. *By Satyadhriti.* Let me have all the glorious irresistible aids of the mighty trio, Mitra, Aryamá, and Varuna.

9. *By Vatsa.* O Indra, possessor of unbounded wealth, the subduer of foes, the lord of horses, may we ever continue to be the celebrators of the praise of such a one as thou art.

PRAPÁTHAKA III.

FIRST DAŚATI.

1. *By Pragátha.* Let these moon-plants fill thee with delight, O holder of the thunderbolt; do thou procure for us wealth, and at the same time kill outright all who hate the Brahmans.

2. *By Viśwámitra.* O Indra, recipient of praise, save us; and since thou art a partaker of our streams of pleasant moon-plant juice, and all our provisions are thy gift, (come to our solemnities).

3. *By Vámadeva (addressed to his sons and grandsons).* Your Indra is the unceasing operative

agent;[1] he is like a constant attendant, a beneficent divinity, worthy of the election of all, ever victorious, the supreme lord.

4. *By Śrutakaksha.* O Indra, let the moon-plant juice flow into thee, as the rivers flow into the sea, since there is no god that surpasses thee.

Rig V. 1 M. 2 A. 4 S. 1 R.
5. *By Madhuchhanda.* The (Sáma Veda) singers with loud songs celebrate Indra; the (Rig Veda) chanters by their sacred verses celebrate Indra; and (the Yajur Veda priests celebrate) Indra with their voices.

6. *By Sukaksha.* May Indra, along with food, give us the treasure of an illustrious and talented progeny; and may he, the fleet divinity, confer upon us horses.

7. *By Gritsamada.* Indra quickly dispels the great fear with which I am seized; for he is unchangeable, and the observer of the actions of men.

8. *By Sanyu.* O recipient of praise, our voices ever encircle thee in every moon-plant sacrifice, as milch-cows do their calves.

9. *By Bharadwája.* O Indra, to obtain thy friendship and our own comfort, we call on thee to come quickly, along with Púshá (the Sun), for the reception of our sacrificial viands.

10. *By Vámadeva.* O Indra, there is no god

---

[1] *i. e.* ever causing strength, food, prosperity, gold, long life.

thy superior, none more powerful than thou art; nor, indeed, O slayer of Vritra, is there one that can be put on a level with thee.

SECOND DAŚATI.

1. *By Virúpa.* I heartily praise thee, the destroyer of the men who hate us, and the unfailing procurer of food and cows.

2. *By Madhuchhanda.* O Indra, let the praises, suited to please, which I have presented, reach thee, the sender down of rain, and lord of all. Rig V. 1 M. 3 A. 2 S. 4 R.

3. *By Vatsa.* It is the man of good morals, and who is without malice, that the Maruts, Aryamá, and Mitra protect.

4. *By Triśoka.* O Indra, wherever, whether in some strong chest or in some hill or well,[1] treasure worthy of regard is laid up, thence do thou bring it to us.

5. *By Sukaksha.* I come to thee, desiring thee to bestow on me great wealth, thou renowned slayer of Vritra, more powerful than any of the race of heroes.

6. *By Vámadeva.* O Indra, we come to thee with stores of sacrificial viands prepared for thee. O brave Śakra, in our most solemn sacrifice, we

---

[1] When the English took Poonah, ten lakhs of rupees belonging to the Peshwa were found built into the side of a well.

come with stores of viands for such a one as thou art.

7. *By Viśwámitra.* O Indra, this morning accept our sacrifice, accompanied with rice, curds,[1] sweet cakes,[2] and praises.

8. O Indra, thou didst with the spray of water cut off the head of the Daitya Namuchi, when thou slewest the rest in the field of battle.

9. *By Vámadeva.* O Indra, these moon-plants, worthy of being subjected to pressure, are pressed for thee. O possessor of immense riches, do thou satisfy thyself with them.

10. *By Vámadeva.* O Indra, possessed of resplendent wealth, these pressed moon-plants are placed for thee on the regularly spread sacred grass: do thou confer happiness on the celebrators of thy praise.

THIRD DAŚATI.

Rig V. 1 M. 7 A. 7 S. 1 R. 1. *By Śunahśepha.* We, thy worshippers,[3] are anxious to drench thee, Indra, the performer of a hundred sacrifices, the lavish bestower of gifts, with our moon-plant juice, as men do the road to the well.[4]

---

[1] The original means sour curds mixed with barley-flour.

[2] Apúpa, the original word, means a cake made of wheat or rice-flour, with butter, and sugar or molasses.

[3] *Or* desirous of food.

[4] Alluding to a custom, still prevalent, of sprinkling daily in the morning the road to the well with cow-dung water.

2. *By Śrutakaksha.* O Indra, come from heaven into our presence with all thy speed, bringing food consisting of viands of a thousand different kinds.

3. *By Triśoka.* The piercer of the clouds,[1] the moment he was born, seizing an arrow, said to his mother, Who are the men of violence, and who the heroes that possess renown?

4. *By Medhátithi.* We call on thee, the much-eulogized and long-armed Indra, for aid,—on thee, the slayer of Vritra, for protection.

5. *By Śaunaka.* Let Varuna, and the sage Mitra, and Aryamá, with the other gods, take delight in us, and lead us in the straight road.

6. *By Vrĭsmátithi.* The goddess Aurora, in the form of the dawn, comes from the distant regions of the moon to this nether world, and diffuses her splendour all around.

7. *By Viśwámitra.* O Mitra and Varuna, performers of meritorious acts, do ye, with showers, irrigate the pasture-lands, and refresh with waters the two worlds.

8. *By Niranyasthúpa.* The sons (of Prishni the Maruts) send forth their voices and the showers from on high, at the time of our sacrifice; and

---

[1] *Or* slayer of Vritra. The whole legend of Vritrásura seems but an allegorical description of the forked lightning passing from one cloud to another, and the other concomitants of a thunder-storm.

desirous of our oblations, they thus act with the greatest readiness, that they may obtain a welcome reception.

Rig V. 1 M. 6 A. 4 S. 17 R. 9. *By Medhátithi.* Vishnu traversed the world, taking but three steps, and covered with his foot this terrestrial world.[1]

FOURTH DAŚATI.

1. *By Medhátithi.* Come hither, O Indra, to me, the preparer of the excellent moon-plant juice, with the readiness thou goest to the other pressers of the plant: drink the moon-plant juice we offer thee.

2. *By Vámadeva.* Why is the praise of him who is of surpassing wisdom, and the mighty god, celebrated by us? That it may be the means of increasing his glory.

3. *By Medhátithi.* The possessor of wealth will not listen to his praise sung by a man who speaks with an indistinct voice, neither will he listen to a murmuring chant, but to hymns distinctly sung.

4. *By Vámadeva.* Indra is greatly celebrated in our eucharistic hymns; he is the giver of food, the lord of provisions, the possessor of the horses named Harí, and the lover of prepared moon-plant juice.

---

[1] There is here an evident allusion to the Váman Avatár and the story of Vishnu's deceiving Bali.

5. *By Śrutakaksha.* Come into our presence to partake of the moon-plant juice and other viands. Do not get angry with us, (but bear with us,) as an elderly man does with a young wife.

6. *By Sumitra.* O possessor of wealth, when is it that praise offered to thee, the lover of glory, is received in the manner that water is taken up by the water-course? It is when we perform our long sacrifice for the obtaining of rain.

7. *By Medhátithi.* Come and drink, throughout Rig V.
all the seasons, the moon-plant juice from the 1 M. 4 A.
Brahmans' golden bowl; for thy friendship prevents 4 S. 5 R.
the shedding of our blood.

8. *By Medhátithi.* O Indra, recipient of praise, we are the persons who extol thee. O drinker of the moon-plant juice, do thou satisfy us with good things.

9. *By Vámadeva.* O Indra, inform us in what sacrifice thou bestowest wealth. O ever-victorious and most awful lord, do thou implant strength in our bodies.

10. *By Śrutakaksha.* O Indra, thou art to be worshipped, because thou lovest the offerer, art courageous, and immoveable, and also because thy heart delights in divine worship.

[End of the first half of the invocation.]

FIFTH DAŚATI.

1. *By Vaśishtha.* O heroic Indra, we praise thee, who art the Sun[1] of this world, the lord of all things animate and inanimate, with the feeling newly calved cows (low for their calves).

2. *By Sanyu.* O Indra, we, the singers of thy praise, invite thee that we may obtain wealth and food; and we, the rest of the priests, call on thee, the protector of holy men, to destroy our enemies, and give us supplies of rain from the clouds.

3. *By Vámadeva.* I praise thee, Indra, the giver of riches; for thou art skilled in all science, liberal to those who sing thy praise, and the possessor of vast riches which thou bestowest in a thousand ways.

4. *By Nandhasa.* We utter praise in the hall of oblation to thee, the supreme lord, who art the destroyer of our foes, the subduer of the hosts of our enemies, who eatest the wealth-conferring sacrificial food with the eagerness that the milch-cow lows for her calf.

5. *By Káleya.* I and my assistant priests, who sing with loud voices during the pressed moon-plant banquet, call for protection on Indra, the acquirer of wealth by his own inherent merit, with

---

[1] *Literally,* "the eye of heaven."

the eagerness the warrior in battle shouts against his opponent.

6. *By Vaśishtha.* The Supreme Artist is willing to give us food along with exalted wisdom;[1] therefore do I with my voice glorify that Indra who is adored by crowds of worshippers, as the carpenter brightens the beauteous wood by planing.

7. *By Medhátithi.* O Indra, drink of our savoury mixed moon-plant juice, satisfy thyself with it, and listen to us in the joyous, prospering, sacrificial assembly, and let thy wisdom aid in preserving us.

8. *By Bharga.* Do thou come to me, the possessor of wisdom, get acquainted with my wealth, rain down blessings on the lovers of cows and the lovers of horses.

9. *By Vaśishtha.* I, Vaśishtha,[2] do not know your movements, nevertheless let the lovely Maruts drink at our moon-plant banquet to-day along with all the gods.

10. *By Pragátha.* Do not celebrate any other god, O my friends: do not destroy yourselves. Praise Indra, the giver of rain, again and again, in

---

[1] *Or* a wife.

[2] The name of Vaśishtha in the text shows plainly, 1st, that the Rishis are the real authors of the Vedas; and, 2ndly, that this text could not have been written long before the time of Ráma Chandra, with whose preceptor, Viśwámitra, the author was contemporary.

the moon-plant sacrifice, and celebrate him in sacred hymns.

SIXTH DAŚATI.

1. *By Puruhanmán.* No foe can by any act slay the offerer of oblations, who by sacrifices makes a friend of Indra, who ever advances his worshippers, is the slayer of every enemy, the mighty, the invincible, and, through innate strength, ever victorious.

2. *By Pragátha.* We praise Indra, the wealthy, the possessor of immense riches; who obliterated the fissure in the Vajra,[1] ever present in sacrifices, when it had been injured by strokes with collar-bones; and again perfectly united it after it had been broken.

3. *By Pragátha.* O flowing-haired Indra, let thy hundreds and thousands of sacrificial-food-loving horses be yoked to the golden chariot, and bring thee to the moon-plant banquet.

4. *By Viśwámitra.* Come, O Indra, with thy sonorously neighing horses, whose hair is marked like peacocks' feathers.[2] Let no one, fowler-like,

---

[1] The word Vajra is usually rendered "thunderbolt." It is a kind of club with a round head filled with spikes. Such a club the Rákshas, at a sacrifice, holds to ward off improper visitants. I have not been able to ascertain any thing further of the legend alluded to in the text.

[2] This seems to lead us to explain Indra's horses to be the rainbow.

dare to entangle thee and prevent thy coming; or, should any one venture to do so, march against him with thy bow, and honour us with thy presence.

5. *By Gautama.* O all-powerful, thou art the god that renders a man truly illustrious. Possessor of wealth, there is no one besides thee that can confer happiness. Indra, I will speak abroad thy praises.

6. *By Purumídha.* Thou, O Indra, art the possessor of food;[1] thou art the superintendent of the purification of moon-plant juice, the lord of bodily strength; thou, single and alone, slayest thy intimidated foes by the many-form, much-praised, warrior-grasped (Vajra).

7. We invite Indra to come to the feast of the gods,—Indra, who is ever ready to proceed to the sacrifice. We invoke Indra, of moon-plant juice-quaffing renown, to stand by us in the battle,—Indra, to give us wealth.

8. *By Medhátithi.* O possessor of untold riches, let the songs of praise in which my friends extol thee meet with acceptance; and do ye who cover up the consecrated viands, my all-glorious learned priests, sing the praises of Indra in eucharistic hymns.

---

[1] *Or* fame.

9. *By Medhátithi.* Truly our sweetest and most melodious notes of praise shall ascend to thee with the celerity of ever-conquering, treasure-bearing, safe-conveying, swift-flying chariots.

10. *By Medhátithi.* As the light coloured (stag),[1] having quitted the desert, approaches the water-pools when thirsty, so do thou come at the time of our banquet, and drink with our wise men.

SEVENTH DAŚATI.

1. *By Bharga.* Furnish us with wealth and all kind of protection; for, O hero, we worship thee, who, like a wealthy man, art the provider of food and the possessor of riches.

2. *By Ritu.* O Indra, bring those provisions they possess from all the wealthy Asurs. O possessor of riches, nourish with them me, the singer of thy praise, and all those who sit on thy regularly disposed sacrificial grass.

3. *By Jamadagni.* Sing ye to the resplendent ones, Mitra, Aryamá (Indra), the conferrer of riches in reward of sacrifice, and Varuna, an adoratory, laudatory, melodious, and eucharistic song.

4. *By Medhátithi.* O Indra, the preparers of the sacrifice, our mighty united band of pathetic singers,

---

[1] Instead of supplying the word *stag*, we may supply *lion*. Both are mentioned in the Bháshya.

unite their voices, inviting thee to the early banquet, accompanied with hymns of praise, and celebrate thee, the god of remote ages.

5. *By Purumedhas.* O etherial priests, do ye extol my sacrificial food to the mighty Indra, who is the slayer of Vritra, the performer of a hundred sacrifices, and is even now ready to strike our cloud-shaped foe with his host-slaughtering thunderbolt.

6. *By Medhátithi.* O etherial priests, do ye celebrate the praises of the mighty Indra, chief among the slayers of our foes, by whom light was produced, the maintainer of sacred rites; who, in union with the god Soma, truly acts the part of a divinity, and who is ever alive to the interests of his worshippers.

7. *Sákti (addresses Indra).* O Indra, do thou, entertaining for us the affection a father does for his son, bring for us wisdom: do thou, the object of worship to adoring multitudes, grant in this sacrificial assembly of the gods, that we, the possessors of natural life, may obtain divine illumination.

8. *By Ibhi.* Do not, O Indra, cast us off; thou art the only source of our delight, and of that of the thousands of animated beings; thou art our protector; thy favour we must obtain. Do not, O Indra, cast us off.

9. *By Medhátithi.* O slayer of our foes, we, the performers of the moon-plant sacrifice, who take our seats on the sacrificial grass along with the sacrifice-consecrating priests, who sing thy praises, encircle thee all around, as the waters do the continental shores.

10. *By Sanyu.* O Indra, bring along with thee whatsoever power and wealth is to be found among the descendants of Nahusha,[1] and other beings, and whatever may be in the five divisions of the earth; and, at the same time, confer on us all bodily strength.

EIGHTH DAŚATI.

1. *By Medhátithi.* Thou, O rainer of blessings, art in truth, whilst our protector, the universal perambulator. O awful god, pourer down of rain, thy voice is heard in the most distant regions, while thy fame is spread abroad in our vicinity, in this lower world.

2. *By Rebhas.* Since, O foe-destroying Indra, always accompanied by thy long-maned horses, thou art omnipotent in the far-distant regions of heaven as well as in the nether sky, the performer of the moon-plant sacrifice continues paying his devotions to thee in hymns of praise.

---

[1] *i. e.* among Rákshasas, Yakshas, and Gandharvas.

3. *By Vatsa.* Extol, with loud voices and feelings corresponding to your words, in the midst of the pleasant banquet of sacred food, the name of Indra, the all-wise hero, the renowned and all-powerful god.

4. *By Sanyu.* O Indra, grant me, for my well-being, an abode composed of the three elements,[1] and the three destinations,[2] and magnificence like that enjoyed by the wealthy; and scatter not such things away from us by thy thunderbolts.

5. *By Trimedhas.* As the rays of light proceed from the Sun as their centre, so are Indra's watery treasures distributed abroad by his mighty power for the benefit of previously subsisting and incipient existences; therefore, as we offer a portion (of sacred food) to the manes of our fathers, so do we offer a portion to him.

6. *By Puruhanmán.* O ever-enduring soul, the man who does not give cannot receive food; but the bountiful man drives his well-matched chariot-horses like Indra, who drives his golden-coloured[3] steeds.

---

[1] *Or* gods, departed spirits, and men; *or* the three qualities of truth, acquisitiveness, and malignity.

[2] *Or* the three fires; *or* the three gods; *or* the three daily sacrifices.

[3] The original word, Harí, means green or golden-coloured. The clouds may be supposed to be Indra's horses, and to them the latter epithet is the more suitable.

7. *By Trimedhas and Purumedhas.* Put on, as your ornament, in every field of battle, the adorable Indra; and do thou, O slaughterer of our foes, ever victorious, worthy of the highest praise, come to partake of the viands offered in our three daily sacrifices.

8. *By Vaśishṭha.* Thou, O Indra, producest the most precious metals, as well as those of inferior value: thine they are, and thou art ever lord paramount over them; but there is nothing that can confer additional dignity on thee, the shepherd of men.

9. *By Pragátha.* What regions art thou traversing? where art thou to be found? for thy spirit is in so many places. O belligerent hero, maker of war, rooter up of thy enemies' cities, wherever thou mayest go, our songs of praise will extol thee.

10. *By Kali.* Here do we this day approach the holder of the thunderbolt. Do ye bring the moon-plant juice for him to-day, and celebrate anew the possessor of all fame.

NINTH DAŚATI.

1. *By Puruhanmán.* I praise that chief of warriors who is the king of men, the performer of journeys in chariots, the incomparable traveller, the subduer of all, the slaughterer of our foes.

2. *By Garbha.* Since, O Indra, we fear thee, do thou render us void of every other fear. O possessor of riches, it is for our preservation we ask this. Do thou, therefore, slay all that hate us, and wish to engage in battle against us.

3. *By Mirí.* O lord of mansions, thou art the supporting beam of our house, the coat of mail of the performer of moon-plant sacrifice, the god who is bedewed with moon-plant juice, the overturner of cities, the lord of many hosts, the bosom-friend of sages.

4. *By Jamadagni.* Truly thou art mighty, O Sun: truly thou art mighty, descendant of Aditi: we adore the splendour of thy essence, thy majesty, and thy glory; for mighty art thou, O divine (Sun).

5. *By Devátithi.* O Indra, thy friend the performer of the moon-plant sacrifice, the possessor of steeds, who drives his chariot and is of the most engaging appearance, is coming with his travelling horses to thy solemn assembly, bringing with him that food thou art ever ready to accept, and with which thy service is always performed.

6. *By Puruhanmán.* O thunderbolt-wielding Indra, were there a hundred heavens, and a hundred earths, and in addition to them a thousand suns, and any other supposable creatures, they could not contain thee; for thou encirclest heaven and earth.

7. *By Devátithi.* Since, O Indra, thou art in-

voked by mankind towards the east, the south, the north, and the west, and art the sender of abundance to multitudes of men, for their children, do thou, illustrious exploder of wind, send abundance to King Turvasa.

8. *By Vaśishtha.* What man is he that can overcome him whose treasure thou, O Indra, art? for, without doubt, possessor of riches, the owner of provisions, who prepares sacrificial viands to obtain heaven, is regarded as peculiarly thine.

9. *By Bharadwája.* O Indra and Agni, the footless Morn is now advancing, outstripping all the tribes of men, and even the Sun himself, with her silver tongue,[1] and swift continued pace, passing over the heavens in thirty steps.[2]

10. *By Medhátithi.* Come close to us, O Indra, bringing with thee the aids resulting from sacrifices to the spirits of the departed. Come, O most felicitous divinity, with those most happy beings to whom we, in a special manner, offer oblations. Come, O Great Father, along with the spirits of our fathers.

TENTH DAŚATI.

1. *By Trimedhas.* We call for protection from hence on thee, the undecaying, the slaughterer of

[1] Alluding to the singing of birds at the dawn.

[2] The thirty Muhúrtas of which a day and night consist.

our foes, the unchangeable, the fleet, the victorious, the slayer of enemies, the famed charioteer, the invulnerable, the increaser of the supplies of water.

2. *By Vaśishtha.* Let not thy usual place of pleasure and relaxation be far distant from our sacrificing priests; but, on the contrary, come from afar to our deity-delighting assembly, and dwell among us and listen to our invocations.

3. *By Vaśishtha.* Offer ye up expressed moon-plant liquor to the moon-plant-drinking, thunderbolt-wielding Indra. Prepare the sacrificial viands for his nourishment, subject them to the necessary purifications, and fill up his joy with the satisfying offerings.

4. *By Sanyu.* We call upon Indra, who is always the slaughterer of our foes, who surveys all creation, is mighty in splendour,[1] of surpassing might, and lord of saints. Be thou present, to exalt us in every conflict.

5. *By Puruchchhesha.* O (sons of Aświni) wealthy through meritorious acts, grant to us as the fruit of our solemn rites, day and night, all we desire, and never by any means destroy our gift, never (destroy) the gift we present to you.

6. *By Vámadeva.* Whenever the priest who chants the sacred verses praises the sender of

---

[1] Or *wrath*.

water,[1] the famous Indra, the supporter of the various kinds of religious rites, let him celebrate his praises in a highly laudatory tone.

7. *By Vatsa.* O Indra, who art a guest at our sacrifice, preserve the sacrificial food with the pleasant moon-plant juice, for thyself, the possessor of the party-coloured horses, the golden Indra, the wielder of the golden thunderbolt.

8. *By Bharga.* Let Indra listen to both our praises and our prayers, till he grant us our desire; and may the ever-moving, the possessor of wealth, who is powerful through merit, come to the moon-plant banquet.

9. *By Pragátha.* O wielder of the thunderbolt, thou art not impoverished by a noble and surpassingly splendid gift, not by one of a thousand pieces' value, no, nor by one of ten thousand; not even, possessor of wealth, by such a gift a hundred times repeated.

10. *By Pragátha.* O Indra, thou abidest more closely by me than a father or a generous brother; thou protectest me like a tender mother; therefore, as thou hast taken up thy abode with us, do thou surround us with all thy wealth.

---

[1] The attentive reader, who can bear the grossness or simplicity of the allusion, will be able to reconcile the translation to the text.

PRAPÁṬHAKA IV.

FIRST DAŚATI.

1. *By Vaśishṭha.* This well-pressed moon-plant juice, mixed with sour curds, is for Indra. O holder of the thunderbolt, come to the sacrificer's house, along with thy pair of horses, to partake of the delight-inspiring banquet.

2. *By Vámadeva.* These moon-plants, accompanied with sacred hymns, are prepared for thy delight, O Indra. Drink the pleasant juice, listen to our songs, and grant the singer his request, O recipient of praise.

3. *By Soma.* I invite Indra to be present with us to-day; for he is the cow producing the water of life, and is manifested in the form of the sacred Brahmanical verse. He is the good milch-cow, the inexhaustible, the provider of provisions for sacrifice, who pours forth large streams of milk, and is richly adorned with ornaments.

4. *By Nodha.* The mighty and inaccessible mountains do not keep thee back, O Indra, when thou comest to confer wealth on one like me, who celebrates thy praise; nor can any thing destroy what has been acquired by thy blessing.

5. *By Medhátithi.* Who, besides me, knows Indra? Do thou, therefore, with thy attendants,

drink my moon-plant juice; for who else prepares the life-giving food? Indra, by his might, beats cities to dust. May he, then, famed for his beautiful countenance, be gratified by our viands.

6. *By Tauraśravasa.* While Indra, the possessor of riches, punishes the neglecters of sacred rites, by driving them beyond the pale of the sacred assembly, let him, at the same time, carry forward our much-desired moon-plant sacrifice to a prosperous issue, for the benefit of our host.

7. *By Twishṭa.* Let the Divine Artist preserve to us the divine gift of speech, and Brahmaṅaspati give us rain, and Aditi save us, and our sons and grandsons, from the malicious violence and reproach of our enemies.

8. *By Vámadeva.* Thou, O giver of riches, art lord supreme, and yet thou regularly findest thy way to the sacrificer's; and the valuable gift sent by thy divine majesty, without fail, reaches its destination.

9. *By Medhátithi.* O Indra, most mighty slaughterer of our foes, possessor of riches, inspirer of dread, do thou yoke thy golden-coloured horses, and come forth with all thy speed into our presence, to drink the moon-plant juice.

10. *By Nrimedha.* O Indra, holder of the thunderbolt, our actively moving fellow-sacrificers are to-day extolling thee: Indra, the offerers of praise

are here; listen to their songs, and come to our abode.

SECOND DAŚATI.

1. *By Vaśishtha.* The Morn, daughter of heaven, now begins to appear, and to advance along with the heavens, shedding her light abroad, subduing with her brilliant eye the mighty power of darkness, and, united with bands of illustrious men, causing the day to shine.

2. *By Vaśishtha.* These heaven-meriting sacrifices call upon you, O twin sons of Aświni, as the cow calls on her calf; and since ye are ready to come to all, ye bestowers of wealth in reward of merit, my soul also calls on you for protection.

3. *By Aświna.* O divine sons of Aświni, who is the man, or where is his abode, who, distressed by destructive famine, has applied to you, and offered up to you sacrifice with moon-plant juice in vain?

4. *By Kutsa.* O twin sons of Aświni, this most pleasant juice of pressed moon-plants is prepared for you in the heaven-meriting sacrifice. Having come this day to our sacrifice, drink of it, O twin sons of Aświni, and afterwards bestow precious gifts on our host, who presides at the solemnities.

5. *By Pragátha.* Ever, by the dripping noise of the moon-plant juice, as well as by articulate sounds, am I inviting thee (O Indra); wherefore, then,

shouldst thou rage at the sacrifice like a fierce lion? for who will not pray to thee, the supreme lord?

6. *By Devátithi.* O officiating priests, Indra wishes to drink the moon-plant juice, and, with his powerful golden-coloured horses yoked to the chariot, the foe-destroyer[1] comes into our presence.

7. *By Vaśishtha.* O wealthy Indra, grant to me, who am of low degree, a large portion; for thou art the possessor of riches, and the god invoked in every war.

8. *By Vaśishtha.* O Indra, I am lord of as many treasures as thou art, and I support him who sings the praises (of the gods). Distributer of wealth, I too give without any evil intention.

9. *By Nrimedha.* Thou, O Indra, art ever ready to slay thy foes, and overcomest all that war against thee. O thou destroyer of the impious, our father, the foe-slaughterer, thou slayest all who wish to slay thee.

10. *By Medha.* Thou, by thy mighty power, slayest thy foes, and from thy heavenly abode, like (a cloud of) dust, envelopest the earth, and with thy embrace surroundest all the world.

---

[1] *Or* cloud-striker; *or* slayer of Vritra.

THIRD DAŚATI.

1. *By Vaśishtha.* I, the preparer of sacrifice for the gods, offer the produce of the cow and other viands, in these solemn rites, to Indra, who, from the first, has been longing for our praise. O possessor of the golden-coloured horses, we acknowledge thee by these oblations, and do thou acknowledge our sacred songs presented to thee along with sweet viands.

2. *By Vaśishtha.* O Indra, worshipped by adoring multitudes, come to the sacred enclosure constructed by the priests in thy hall. Since thou art our protector and nourisher, grant us wealth, and satisfy us with moon-plant juice.

3. *By Gritsamada.* He who rends the clouds and creates the waters, who is the sender and restrainer of rain, and the giver of gifts, is Indra, who forms the mighty clouds, and sends down torrents of water, is the bestower of blessings, and the undecaying god.

4. O Indra, possessor of riches, we, when preparing the moon-plants, praise thee; and thee we praise while presenting the offering of sacred food. Bring thou for us a posterity possessed of wealth derived from thee, and grant that through thy protection we may be enabled to keep our inferiors in subjection and conquer our enemies.

5. *By Sahago.* We, who are eager for the possession of riches, take hold of thy right hand, O Indra, lord of wealth. We know thee, O mighty god, to be lord of cattle; give us then that wealth which consists in cows that yield large supplies of milk.

6. *By Vaśishťha.* Men call on Indra while engaged in war, that they may obtain merit, and thus insure success. Do thou grant (Indra) to the illustrious attendants on the sacrifice, that they may have their cow-houses filled with desirable cows.

7. *Gaurivíti.* O ye fleet rays, that, like birds, ascend to the seat of your lord, that delight in sacrifice, survey all things, and present our petitions, do ye veil the waters, and dissipate the darkness, grant us clear vision, and release us from the snare in which we are entangled.

8. *By Vena.* Those who from their hearts desire union with the Divine Being, in the heavens in the bosom of Yama, look with steady vision to thee, glorious in thy gait and in thy goings forth with golden plumage, the messenger of Varuna, the powerful, the magnificent.

9. *By Kula.* The first-born glorious Brahma has, from of old, shed abroad his brilliant rays to the utmost bounds of space, and now sheds them abroad to the regents of all the different points in the heavens, which are the reducers to

form of this world, and every where residing in the wombs of truth and falsehood.[1]

10. *By Suhotra.* Let all newly invented and all long approved delight-conferring hymns of praise be sung in honour of the mighty, the heroic, the powerful, the foe-destroying, large-bodied god, who is the holder of the thunderbolt, and the ancient of days.

FOURTH DAŚATI.

1. *By Dyutana.* The water that resides in the river Anśumatí,[2] dark by its whirlpools, resembling moon-plant juice, and to be approached only with tens of thousands of followers, came to Indra, the subduer of foes by accumulated merit, when he stopped the slaughtering army by the river's current; for Indra regards with favour the performers of sacred rites.

2. *By Dyutana.* O Indra, when fleeing from Vritrásura's wrath, all the gods, thy friends, deserted thee; thou alone, with the Maruts,[3] didst conquer the enemy's army. Let thy friendship be manifested to us.

3. *By Brihadukta.* I praise the sustainer of the world, him who laid hold of the whole multitude of

---

[1] *Truth and falsehood* means the present mixed state of things.

[2] The Yamuná.

[3] The winds.

his herd of cattle during the conflict, who, though aged, is ever young. Behold the wisdom of the god Indra; even at this day it is he who stops the breath of life.[1]

4. *By Dyutana.* O Indra, thou becamest the conferrer of happiness when brought forth by the seven friendly (Rishis). Then didst thou from thy hiding-place manifest thyself to the heavens and to the earth, and enter the field of battle, for the benefit of the inhabitants of the terrestrial and celestial regions.

5. *By Vámadeva.* I praise thee, the holder of the thunderbolt, thee who speakest like the god of eloquence, who wearest the crown, the possessor of immense wealth, the lord of all, the constant participator in our sacrifices, the dweller in heaven, and slayer of the cloud-shaped demon Vritra. Desirous of circumventing (mine enemies), I praise thee, the lord supreme, and slayer of foes.

6. *By Vaśishṭha.* As for you (my priests), do ye bring offerings for the mighty one, who, for his intellectual benefit, greatly exalts the sacrificer; and, at the same time, sing your best songs of praise: and as for thee, O satisfier of the wants of mankind, do thou come to our people who are stationed all around.

---

[1] Meaning that the age of miracles and *Herculean* labours is past, and God is now known by his providence.

7. *By Viśwámitra.* In this war, I call on Indra, the conferrer of happiness, the possessor of wealth, the greatest of heroes, who hears our prayers, and is most forward to confer on us the provisions of our foes, and to aid us in battle; for he is the slayer of our enemies, and the victorious spoiler of their wealth.

8. *By Vaśishṫha.* O Vaśishṫha, do thou send sacrificial viands to Indra, and praise him in the war; for it is he who, by his might, every where preserves all religious rites, and is the hearer of our praises, which we cause to ascend from every quarter.

9. *By Gauri.* This circle,[1] fixed in the waters, and growing up to the very heavens, solicits for the inhabitants of this world the sweet aqueous liquid, which resides in the rays of light, and which Indra gives forth for the supply of food.

FIFTH DAŚATI.

1. *By Tárkshya.* I, Tárkshya, call on the provider of food, the leader of the gods, who exists by his own power, the destroyer of our enemies' chariots, who is possessed of the indestructible thunderbolt, the victorious in the field of battle,

[1] The Brahmanical emblem of Vishnu. Here the rainbow is meant.

the ever-moving Indra, to come quickly hither for our ease and happiness.

2. *By Garga.* I call, in every contest, on Indra the deliverer, the preserver, who deserves to be specially invoked, the heroic, the powerful, who is adored by all the numerous tribes of men. Let that wealth-possessing Indra partake of our offering.

3. *By Vemada.* We worship Indra, who grasps with his right hand the thunderbolt, the driver of the excellent, manœuvre-performing gold-coloured horses, who causes the hair of his foes to stand on end through terror, and inspires them with dread by his armies seizing their wealth.

4. *By Vámadeva.* We worship Indra, who ever slays his foes, and ever subdues them like a mighty hero, (Indra) the great, the unequalled, the supreme, the eminent holder of the Vajra, the slayer of the cloud-shaped demon, the accepter of the sacrificial food, the giver of wealth, the wealthy, the possessor of excellent precious stores.

5. *By Vámadeva.* The man who slays us and bestows our goods on others, and who, though a murderous wretch, boasts of his liberality, I will destroy, O Indra, either in battle or by my bodily strength. This I am determined to execute through thy aid, O supreme lord.

6. *By Vámadeva.* It is Indra whom warriors invoke when engaged with their enemies, and whom

those who bound along in chariots, those who stand in the field of battle, and those who desire rain invoke, and whom the learned Brahmans supply with their offerings.

7. *By Viśwámitra.* O Indra and Parvata, come in your spacious chariot to the house of him who invites you to the acceptable sacrificial viands; of him who, with his sons and grandsons, partakes of the sacred food. O ye gods, praised in hymns and satisfied with food, grow great by the offerings presented in our sacrifice.

8. *By Rinu.* (The worshipper) sends up many collected hymns of praise, for the obtaining of water, to Indra, who from the top[1] of the skies, turning round on all sides, renders the heaven and earth stable, as (the carpenter does) the wheels of a chariot by joining them to the axle.

9. *By Vasu.* Truly these, my friends, come into close contact with thee by their friendly offices; do thou, therefore, the possessor of water, come to us in floods, advancing, most wise lord, with the speed a son comes to save his father, while protecting the accumulated household treasures.

10. *By Gautama.* Who is the first of men? It is he who strengthens by food the hard-working, foe-scorning, rampant, rain-dispensing, delight-con-

---

[1] *Literally*, the root.

ferring cattle attached to the pole of Indra's chariot.

[End of the verses in the Trishtup measure.]

SIXTH DAŚATI.

Rig V. 1 M. 3 A. 3 S. 1 R.

1. *By Madhuchhanda.* The (Sáma Veda) singers sing thy praise, the (Rig Veda) chanters chant to the god of song, and the officiating (Yajur Veda) priests extol thee, O Indra, the performer of a hundred sacrifices, with the eagerness they extol their ancestors.[1]

2. *By Yata.* Let every voice extol Indra, who is diffused on every side like the ocean,[2] is the most excellent conductor of chariots, lord of food, and the protector of holy men.

3. *By Gautama.* O Indra, drink this ancient, immortality-conferring, moon-plant juice, the intoxicator of Śukra.[3] Let the sacrificial streams flow into thee in the sacred enclosures.

---

[1] *Or* as dancers raise their dancing-pole. [2] *Or* the sky.

[3] The story of Śukra's drunkenness is given at length in the Matsya Purána. Completely to destroy and prevent the resuscitation of Kacha, the son of Vrihaspati, the Asuras killed him, burnt him, and mingled his ashes with spirits, which they made Śukra drink. But it was of no avail. Śukra revived Kacha in his own belly, taught him the resuscitative Mantra, had himself ripped up, Kacha taken out, and his own life again restored by the Mantra. Annoyed, it is said, at this transaction, he cursed all drinkers of spirits.

4. *By Atri.* O variegated Indra, there is nothing in my house worthy of being presented to thee. O thunderer, possessor of wealth, convey to us riches with both thy hands.

5. *By Tiraśchi.* O Indra, hear the invocation of me the brave, moon-plant sacrifice-performing Tiraśchi, who comes as thy suppliant. Satisfy me with wealth, for thou art of a noble disposition.

6. *By Gautama.* O Indra, subduer of thy foes, powerful god, let the pressed moon-plants yield satisfaction to thy senses, as the Sun does by his rays to the world under his influence.

7. *By Medhátithi.* Come, O Indra, possessor of brilliant treasures, with thy golden-coloured horses, down from thy heavens to our concert, excellent as that of the Rishi Kańwa, and then proceed from this world to the heavens of the supreme ruler.

8. *By Tiraśchi.* O worthy of all praise, let our eucharistic songs fix thee, as firmly as the charioteer is fixed in his seat, and let their symphony sound before thee, like the lowing of newly calved cows for their calves.

9. *By Viśwamanas.* We desire to praise that Indra who mightily exalts his worshippers with pacificatory songs and sacred verses. May he, the quaffer of the sacred mixed moon-plant juice, drink even to repletion.

10. *By Sanyu.* O wealthy Indra, who art su-

perior to all in riches, and possessest the largest store of sacred viands, lord of the food offered to the manes, this pressed moon-plant juice is prepared for thee: drink of it even to repletion.

SEVENTH DAŚATI.

1. *By Bharadwája.* Bring all the vessels; for the wise Indra, who desires our drink-offerings, is a heroic god, the mighty traverser of space, going forth and returning back again.

2. *By Vámadeva.* Thou didst utterly contemn the fixed cloud (Vritra) reposing on the mountain top, and the mighty sacrificer, and the harsh words of thy foes.

3. *By Priyamedha.* We engage in thy worship, O Indra, of great bodily might, to obtain thy succour. Increase thou our happiness progressively, like the motion of a chariot; for thou art the performer of many meritorious acts, the subduer of armies, and the protector of holy men.

4. *By Pragátha.* He holds the first place among the wealthy, who renders himself conspicuous by the performance of sacrifice, and whom Indra, our patriarch and father, through whose favour the means of performing sacrifice are procured, renders conspicuous among the gods.

5. *By Vámadeva.* Wherever the swift brilliant

horses carry thee in thy chariot, there they drink the pleasant sweet juice, and there they prepare the sacred provisions.

6. *By Sanyu.* I praise thee the indestructible, the lord of strength, the subduer of all, the hero, thee who art possessed of stores of provisions, and the possessor of all knowledge.

7. *By Vámadeva.* I celebrate the tamer of multitudes of horses, and his victorious fleet horses. May he bestow on us all the excellent things that occasion happiness, and preserve our lives.

8. *By Jetá.* It is Indra who was the destroyer of the cities of the Asuras, who is ever young, who is of incalculable might, the sustainer of all the works of man, the holder of the thunderbolt, and the recipient of the praises of myriads.

EIGHTH DAŚATI.

1. *By Pramedha.* I offer, with all my heart, the thrice-sacred song of praise to the all-resplendent lord, while my friend, with all his skill, serves him in performing the sacrifice and presenting the offering.

2. *By Kaśyapa.* Indra's pair of courageous horses are said to belong to the creation of the all-wise Kaśyapa, through whom all our rites and sacrifices become glorious.

3. *By Priyamedha.* O my friends, praise ye—O sons of Priyamedha, praise Indra, and let his grandsons also join in praising him, with all the fire a mighty man displays in attacking a powerful enemy.

Rig V. 1 M. 3 A. 3 S. 5 R. 4. *By Madhuchhanda.* We offer the eucharistic magnifying song of praise to Indra, the rebuker of hosts of foes, with the affection that that mighty god rejoices in our moon-plant offerings and friendship.

5. *By Priyamedha.* I call on you, the lord of all, the preserver of strength undiminished, and of all other desirable things, for the protection of our footmen and charioteers.

6. *By Bharadwája.* He who with all his heart praises the indestructible hero is the man who subdues his foes, and who, glorious in himself, escapes, through thy aid, from every formidable enemy, and from all sin.

7. *By Atri.* O Indra, our lord, the performer of merit-conferring acts, bestow on us large gifts from thy treasures. Above all things, O all-surveying and most bountiful divinity, grant us wealth.

8. *By Praskańwa.* Like the swift-moving birds at the refulgent dawn, thou visitest all the biped and quadruped tribes, and movest through all the stages of time, encircling the whole heavens.

9. *By Trita.*[1] O all ye gods that are stationed in the shining firmament of heaven, this long-continued invocation is addressed to you, from the place where there is a sincere offerer, and the water of life prepared for you.

10. We are worshipped in chanted hymns and songs of praise by him who performs these rites. He is presenting a sacrifice for the gods in the brilliant assembly of priests.

NINTH DAŚATI.

1. *By Triśoka.* All the armies and heroes come together to Indra, the subduer of our foes, the indestructible, the inspirer of awe, the possessor of great bodily strength, the fleet, the preserver. Prepare and offer up the excellent glorious sacrifice in the sacred place.

2. *By Sumedha.* I offer sacrifice to thee, the chief of the shining hosts. Thou slewest the cloud-shaped demon, and dispersedst water for the benefit of mankind. The two shining worlds and the earth

[1] To explain this and the next *Rich*, the Bháshya gives the following legend. "Ápta Rishi had three sons: in returning late from a sacrifice one of them either fell, or was driven by his brothers, into a dry well. There, without any materials, he goes through in imagination all the forms of a sacrifice, invoking especially Vrihaspati, who invokes the gods, and induces them to accept his offering and deliver him."

come to thee with fear and awe, on account of thy might, holder of the thunderbolt.

3. *By Vámadeva.* Come all of you and join in praising him, who, on account of his might, is lord of heaven, who alone is honoured as a guest by all men. Anxiously desirous to come to the newly prepared sacrifice, he proceeds the first to the place where the solemnities are being conducted.

4. *By Satya.* O Indra, recipient of the praises of myriads, meeting no obstruction, do we approach thee. O possessor of much wealth, and worthy to be extolled, there is no one worthy of praise equal to thee, who graciously delightest in our eucharistic hymns, as a man delights in the praises of his friend.

5. *By Viśwámitra.* Our many faultless songs are daily sung to extol Indra, the supporter of mankind, the wealthy, the causer of increase, who is worshipped by myriads, is immortal, and worthy to be extolled by all.

6. *By Krishta.* Your heaven-directed minds, all ascending in union, and desirous (of his favour), praise Indra, and depend on him, the wealthy son of Aditi, for protection, as a wife does on her husband.

7. *By Angina.* Do ye satisfy with delight that Indra who assumed the shape of a ram, who is invoked by myriads and praised in songs, the ocean

of wealth, to whom the two worlds go in suppliant guise, the almighty, the beloved. Extol ye him, the possessor of wisdom, that ye may obtain happiness.

8. *By Satya.* Worship the ram[1] who inhabits heaven, whom many unite by praising him in hundreds of songs; and forward the sacrificial viands, as men do grain to their horses, along with faultless hymns to that Indra, who comes in his sacrifice-going chariot, in order to afford us protection.

9. *By Bharadwája.* The mighty earth which receives the water for the sustenance of all beings, the two worlds, the distillers of water and of excellent form, dissolve through the operation of Varuna into the form of watery torrents, and yet continue free from all decay.

10. *By Medhátithi.* O Indra, thou diffusest water through the two worlds as the morn diffuses light. The excellent goddess mother produced thee to be the lord of the heavenly hosts and the illustrious ruler over men.

11. *By Kutsa.* Worship ye in songs of praise the joyful Indra, who propels the dark pregnant clouds with rapid motion; for, anxious for water,

---

[1] *i. e.* Indra; see the preceding *Rich;* and consider how far this may be connected with the horned Egyptian god, and the first sign in the Ecliptic.

we call on the sender of rain, who holds the thunderbolt in his right hand, and is the lord of the Maruts, in order that we may enjoy his friendship.

[End of the verses in the Anashtup metre.]

TENTH DAŚATI.

1. *By Nárada.* Indra goes to the place where are pressed moon-plants; for he is of a noble disposition, and knows what kind of a sacrifice is there offered up by me the extoller of the gods.

2. *By Gośukti and Aśwaśukti.* Sing ye songs with your voices to Indra, who is worshipped by myriads and praised by myriads. Come ye, and sit as suppliants before the mighty one.

3. O holder of the thunderbolt, we speak in honour of thee, the possessor of all joy, the sender of rain, the subduer of hosts, and the fashioner of worlds.

4. *By Parvata.* Because, O Indra, accompanied by Vishnu, by Trita, Ápta, and the Maruts, thou drinkest to satisfaction of the moon-plant juice, we worship thee.

5. *By Viśwamanas.* O sacrificing priests, pour out the juice that inspires delight[1] more than alcohol, (and serve it up) along with the sacrificial

---

[1] *Or* more intoxicating.

viands; for it is intended for the hero who ever prospers those who celebrate his praise.

6. *By Viśwamanas.* Do ye pour out the pleasant moon-plant juice; for the god sends us wealth in abundance, impelled by his own benevolent disposition.

7. *By Viśwamanas.* O my friends, let us praise Indra, the hero who is worthy of all praise, who singly subdues all the hosts of his enemies.

8. *By Nrimedha.* Sing loud songs of praise to the mighty and wise Indra, the creator of food, the possessor of knowledge, who thirsts for your praises.

9. He who alone gives wealth in abundance to the man who performs sacrifice, is the invincible lord, Indra.

10. *By Viśwamanas.* O my friends, we pray to Indra, the holder of the thunderbolt, for food. I praise him who acts most humanely towards you, and subdues our foes.

PRAPÁṬHAKA V.

FIRST DAŚATI.

1. *By Pragátha.* O Indra, in this assemblage of the gods, I praise that incomparable strength of thine by which thou slewest the cloud-shaped demon.

2. *By Bharadwája.* It is the spirit of that same pressed moon-plant which, when thou hadst quaffed,

thou slewest (the giant) Śambara, that I now offer thee. Drink of it, therefore, O Indra.

3. *By Nrimedha.* O ever-victorious and most meritorious, come to us; for, like a mountain, thou presentest thy huge front on every side, and art lord of the heavens.

4. O most powerful Indra, we desire that joyous sensation, which, arising from plenteous potations of the moon-plant juice, delights the mind, and under the influence of which thou slewest the cannibal Atrina.

5. *By Irimiri.* O descendant of Aditi, worthy to receive oblations, cause that our lives may be lengthened so that we may enjoy long life: favour our descendants, and increase our property.

6. *By Viśwamanas.* O thou, in whose hand is the thunderbolt, assure us of the dispersion of the band of death-bringing demons, in the same manner as the rising Sun daily assures us that all the animated tribes will disperse themselves abroad.

7. *By Irimiri.* O Son of Aditi, thou drivest away disease and every hurtful and malicious foe: do thou separate us from every thing that is sinful.

8. *By Vaśishṭha.* O Indra, drink the moon-plant juice; and let that delight thee, O possessor of the golden-coloured horses, which I, the director of the sacrifice, have ordered to be bruised with stones, by

the arms of the officiating priests, joined together like yoked horses.

SECOND DAŚATI.

1. *By Saubhari.* O Indra, thou art united in family and associated in war with him who is without enmity and free from sin, and with such thou choosest the closest alliance.

2. *By Saubhari.* O my friends, I praise that Indra, whose coming has long been greatly desired by you and by us, that he may grant us protection.

3. *By Saubhari.* Come to our sacrifice, permit no calamity to befall us, stand not at a distance, O Maruts, who march in opposition to our foes, who shine forth with equal lustre, and who destroy the powerful hosts of our adversaries.

4. *By Saubhari.* Lord of horses, lord of cows, and lord of earth, come to this splendid sacrifice. Lord of the moon-plant, drink thou of the moon-plant juice.

5. *By Prayága.* O our lord, united to thee we can speak with him who breathes out threatenings against us, and stand in the battle against the cow-stealing tribe.

6. *By Saubhari.* As are the rays of light, so are ye, O Maruts, all of equal splendour, united as brothers in the closest family bond, and inhabitants

of all quarters of the world. Support, in a body, the performers of sacrifice.

7. *By Nrimedha.* O Indra, full of merit, and observer of all things, bring us strength, bring us wealth, and heroes who will crush our foes in battle.

8. *By Nrimedha.* O Indra, worthy of all praise, we pray to thee for all desirable things, and prepare for thee this sacrifice with the zeal the merchant embarks on the waters.

9. *By Saubhari.* O Indra, while in thy presence, we utter praises to thee, collected, as birds in their roost, to drink sweet inebriating, eloquence-inspiring[1] juice mixed with the produce of the cows.

10. *By Saubhari.* O holder of the thunderbolt, like to whom none previously existed, we who desire the favour of the gods, and are like those who forward carts of grain, invoke thee, possessed of variegated splendour.

THIRD DAŚATI.

1. *By Gotama.* The delightsome brilliant rays of light, which accompany the rain-dispelling lord, drink the delicious, sweet, all-pervading (juice)

---

[1] Those who have heard sung the praises of the juice of the grape, or of the barley-bree, will not mistake the meaning of this epithet.

offered in this sacrifice, and satisfy all the world under their dominion.

2. *By Mada.* The Brahman is preparing, according to the instituted form, the increase-causing juice contained in the delight-inspiring moon-plant; therefore, O possessor of great bodily strength, grasper of the thunderbolt, send down the moving heavens, and disperse the rain-bearing clouds over all thy dominions.

3. *By Gotama.* We call on that Indra, who grows great by the sweet moon-plant juice, and who, through his might, slays Vritra and all our foes, that he may come to our protection in our great wars, and preserve us in every lesser conflict.

4. *By Gotama.* O Indra, grasper of the thunderbolt, the bruisers of the moon-plant celebrate thy unequalled strength, by which, united with wisdom, thou didst slay the crafty Mrigásur, thus conferring a blessing on thy dominions.

5. *By Gautama.* Come, O Indra, with speed, and subdue and trample (our foes) under-foot, since thy Vajra is irresistible. To thee belong wealth and power; therefore slay the cloud-shaped demon, and supply us with water, blessing thy dominions.

6. *By Gautama.* When, O Indra, those who come to worship invoke thee, and delight thee with sacrificial viands, and ceremonies used for the obtaining victory over our enemies, then do thou

yoke thy banquet-going horses, and having slain some one and seized his wealth, bestow it on us.

7. *By Gautama.* The beloved (manes of our ancestors), which before were trembling through hunger, have now eaten and are satisfied. They are the subject of our praise, they shine by unborrowed light, are most wise, and celebrated by all minds capable of eulogizing their actions. O Indra, yoke thy golden-coloured horses.

8. *By Gautama.* O Indra, possessor of wealth, come and listen to our songs; be not like those who speedily depart. Whenever thou art ready to enrich us the moon-plant offerers, and art desirous of sacrifices, yoke thy two golden-coloured horses.

9. *By Gautama.* The moon, surrounded by rays of light, and encircled by the waters, holds its constant course in the heavens. O golden-wheeled lightnings, men do not always gaze on you, admiring your speed. O heaven and earth, hear the praises I offer.

10. *By Ausasyu.* O twin sons of Aświni, the Rishi who celebrates your praise adorns with eucharistic hymns your beloved, rain-causing, wealth-conveying chariot; therefore do ye, rendered joyous by our liquors, listen to my invitation.

FOURTH DAŚATI.

1. *By Vatsa.* O Agni, we light thee up into a flame by our praises, till thy sacred wood illuminates the heavens. Bring thy glorious, inexhaustible store of provisions for our praise-chanting priests.

2. *By Vatsa.* We invoke thee, O Agni,[1] the inviter of the gods, who sittest on the cut Kuśa grass, and art possessed of pure radiance. I invite thee to the spread out seat of Kuśa grass, to partake of our inebriating liquors in this sacrifice.

3. *By Vatsa.* May the resplendent daughter of the Sun arouse us to obtain wealth, as she aroused the king Satyaśrava, of noble lineage, who delighted in horses.

4.[2] Bestow on us a good and auspicious intellect, along with wisdom and food, that we may secure thy friendship; and do thou delight in our spirituous liquors, as cows do in rich pasturage.

5. We reverently approach thee for food to support our strength, and to obtain good fortune, O thou mighty one, of beautiful aspect, possessor of

[1] I have been compelled to translate here an accusative by a vocative, on account of the occurrence of the pronoun *thee*.

[2] The name of the Rishi is only once mentioned after this in the Bháshya; whether for the reason mentioned in the Preface, or from some omission in the work, or in my copy, I cannot determine.

the golden-coloured horses, and who holdest the steel Vajra in both thy hands.

6. He who causes the well-filled golden-coloured horses' grain-dish to glisten, is the man who will stand in the first place before thy rain-causing, cow-conferring chariot. O Indra, now yoke thy horses.

7. Daily, in the evening, do we reverently adore that Agni, who, with the alacrity that cows and fleet horses in the evening come to their homes, confers upon us wealth. Bring here food for those who celebrate thy praises.

8. Aryamá, Mitra, and Varuna,[1] gods of the same race, do not embrace vile death-bringing sin, and they utterly disperse our foes.

FIFTH DAŚATI.

1. The sweet juice of the Soma goes to Indra, Mitra, Pushá, and Bhaga. Wherefore, Indra, and all ye gods, drinkers of the pressed-moon juice, go to the auspicious sacrifice.

2. Thou comest with alacrity for the reception of our sacred viands; thou slayest our malicious foes, and when we flee, thou comest to save us.

3. O mighty Soma,[2] father of the gods, all-

[1] These are forms of the Sun, as also Pushá and Bhaga, mentioned next *Rich*.

[2] The moon-plant personified, and considered as the original essence, and all-pervading spirit.

diffusive as the sea, do thou come to this holy place.

4. O Soma, our purifier, fleet as a horse, come and bestow on us auspicious wealth.

5. The divine Soma, graceful and wise, was produced in the presence of the sacrificial liquids to cause joy and confer renown.

6. We ply thee with the pressed moon-plant juice for the furtherance of the renowned Brahmanical sacrifice; for, O hero famed for alacrity, thou art the provider of all kinds of food.

7. Dost thou not know the heroic Maruts, visible in their own place of abode, the children of Rudra with splendid horses?

8. O Agni, to-day we seek to please thee, the auspicious, the heart-delighting, with praises and offerings in the sacrificial hall, as men by food try to please their horses.

9. (O Soma), the priestly chanters approach thee for food, with the alacrity that the swift horses of the all-preserving god mount the heavens.

10. O mighty Soma, our purifier, come quickly to the famous sweet libation; for thou art the lord of the singers of the sacred hymns.

SIXTH DAŚATI.

1. O constant bestower of gifts, bring to us riches of all kinds; for this we pray to thee, O possessor of all might.

2. I, the sacrifice-superintending priest, praise the well-known illustrious Indra.

3. The priests worship Indra with hymns of praise, extolling him, that he may confer on them gifts and slay their foes.

4. O praised by myriads, the carpenter[1] made the chariot for thy horses, and the artist god made for thee the glittering thunderbolt.

5. Indra, when his worship is neglected, neither provides a happy place of abode, nor riches, nor so much as permits us to touch for distribution any part of his much-desired treasures.

6. The pure, all-sustaining, divine rays of light[2] remain ever without fault.

7. Come, O Indra, with all thy bands, like the herd of cows collected in the cow-house.

8. O Indra, we who dwell in the hall, where the sweet juice is placed, satisfy thee with it, and meditate on thy wealth.

9. The priests, with their auspicious incantations,

---

[1] *i. e.* Viśwakarma.

[2] The word *Go*, here translated "rays of light," may also mean cows, voices, or waters.

worship Arka;[1] and Indra, renowned and ever young, receives their praise.

10. Sing a song of praise to the sage Indra, most renowned for slaughtering our foes, and in whose worship you are now engaged.

SEVENTH DAŚATI.

1. The consumer, the sacrifice-presenting Agni, knows all things, is indeed the very chariot of wisdom.

2. *By Gaupáyana.* O Agni, thou art to us the chief of the gods, our saviour, the conferrer of bliss, the subject of our highest praises.

3. Agni, like the Sun with his variegated colours, possesses the jewels of all the earth's mighty ones.

4. Thou wast, from the beginning, the recipient of the praise of all, and thou art still, doubtless, the same to the inhabitants of this world.

5. The goddess of the morn, of distinguished birth, acts towards the much-celebrated night as towards a sister.

6. In whatever place we provide the materials for sacrifice, there Indra and all the gods present themselves.

7. As many by-paths meet in the highway, so let all riches meet in thee.

---

[1] The Sun.

8. We, the possessors of heroic sons, destined to live a hundred winters,[1] obtain the food placed here by the gods, and are filled with joy.

9. The Goddess of Water, and Mitra, and Varuna, are making the grain to swell; therefore, O Indra, send us plenty of solid food.

10. Indra appears glorious throughout all the world.

EIGHTH DAŚATI.

1. The mighty (Indra), possessed of vast strength, amid the threefold songs of praise drank to his heart's content from the vessel containing the liquor mixed with barley, and was well satisfied with the pressed moon-plant juice prepared by the priests. When he, mighty hero, had thus been rendered cheerful and fitted for the performance of mighty acts, he slew the huge giant. Then the faithful divine Soma, and the faithful divine Indra, mutually embraced each other.

2. Indra, who watches over the thousands of human beings, the intelligence of the wise, the all-glorious, the performer of many religious acts, the mighty hero, who knows the dwelling of the Morn,

---

[1] In the ancient Scandinavian poems time is also reckoned by winters. We see also that in the time of the Rishis, one hundred years was the utmost extent of human life, by the confession of the Veda itself.

sends forth the purifying, life-giving, clear, earth-born waters.

3. Come, O Indra, from a distance to us, let the preserver of holy men encircle our sacrifice, and let the lord of saints act as the king who resides in many palaces. We, who are engaged in the moon-plant sacrifice, call on the mighty hero to receive our viands, as sons call on a father to receive the food offered to the manes.

4. I invoke Indra, the possessor of wealth, the ever faithful supporter of holy men, against whom no one can bring any accusation. Do thou labour with him who is the most liberal bestower of riches, and who is worshipped with songs of praise. May the grasper of the thunderbolt smooth all our paths for the attainment of wealth.

5. O Agni, whom I now place in thy sacred southern recess, hear the sacred consecratory verses. O Indra and Váyu, I invoke you two to grant me divine strength, I invoke you that you may confer on me new and excellent gifts, since you are the principal agents in the world, who reside every where, and fill the vault of heaven: for assuredly all our sacrifices ascend into the presence of the gods, as do the different Maruts.

6. Our intellects, strengthened by holy songs, approach the mighty Vishnu and the Marudgana; and with such a mind, I, Marut, come for super-

natural might, to enable me to offer sacrifice, to confer on me happiness, and render my offerings propitious, and for power to carry on the sacrifice I purpose to perform.

7 The purifying (Agni), encircled by his white radiance, along with his attendant priests, escapes from all sin; and like the Sun, when, with his attendant rays, all pure, and red, and brilliant, he shines out from behind the rainy cloud, thou, with thy seven hymning priests, encirclest all created forms.

8 I worship the god Savitá, parent of heaven and earth, who superintends the sacrifices of the wise, who makes sacred rites to prosper, who bestows gifts, is altogether lovely by the possession of intelligence, and whose radiance from on high, through the words of the wise, shines around the place of the sacrifice, whilst the golden-handed performer of merit-conferring deeds proceeds to the heaven of mercy.

9 I meditate on Agni, the inviter of the gods to the sacrifice, the giver of wealth, the son of strength, the possessor of wealth, possessed of wisdom equal to a Brahman, who goes aloft, is a god manifested in the form of the propitious sacrifice, the light of the other gods, mercy itself, shining on all sides by means of the brilliant flame-causing liquid, and the oblation of clarified butter.

10. That extraordinary feat was thine, O Indra, that man-preserving deed in former times celebrated in heaven. Thou, with thy divine power, art the slayer of the Asuras, thou art the performer of every pious act. Supply us, along with strength, with all things suitable for mortals. O performer of many sacrifices, supply us with food in abundance

[End of the verses in praise of Indra.]

NINTH DAŚATI.

[What follow are the verses used for consecration of the liquid.]

1. The holy ground daily receives the sacrificial viands for thee, (O Agni, receives) that strengthening, adorable, most excellent food.

2. O Soma, do thou consecrate, for the drinking of Indra, the pressed moon-plant juice, by the flavouring, inebriating, dripping process of distillation.[1]

3. O sprinkler of water, consecrate the inebriating juice for the Marudgana, who sustain all things by their might.

4. Consecrate for thyself that inebriating liquor, which satisfies the gods, and destroys the eulogists of sin.

5. The maker of the sacrifice sends up this three-

[1] The distillation here mentioned is merely a dripping of juice. No heat is applied.—See Preface.

fold supplication; then, with the eagerness cows low for their calves, Indra comes with the hoarse-sounding thunders.

6. Consecrate for Indra and the Marudgana the strongly inebriating moon-plant juice, and I will seat myself by the womb[1] of the shining divinity.

7. He seats himself near the resplendent moon-plants sedulously purified with water, with the agility that the mountain-hawk seats himself on his perch.

8. O Indra, consecrate the spirituous liquor prepared by our active exertions, for the drinking of the gods, and the Marudgana, and Váyu.

9. The mountain-produced, pressed moon-plant is distilling its juice in the holy place. Thou, O Soma, art the embroiler of all things in thy drunken frolics.[2]

10. The greatly beloved, the heavenly, the learned, the wise director of the sacrifice, placed by the rites of consecration in heaven and earth, throughout the whole period of his existence, comes to us by means of the pressed moon-plant sacrifice.

---

[1] The vessel in which the liquor ferments, and the alcoholic part is produced.

[2] *Or* when in thy cups, the sustainer of all things.

TENTH DAŚATI.

1. The moon-plants distilled by me to procure for us food, and the pressed plants of the rich institutors of these sacrificial rites, have gone up to the sacrificial banquet.

2. O Brahmans, the copious supplies of the moon-plant furnish us abundance of liquid; as the buffaloes bring to us abundance of wealth.

3. O sender of rain, consecrate the pressed moon-plants, make us renowned in the world, and utterly slay all that hate us.

4. O sender of rain, O holy one, thou art closely united to the Sun. We invoke thee, thou most bright eye of heaven.

5. The consecrated, animating, dearly loved, poet-inspiring moon-plant is preparing with the celerity that the charioteer gets ready his horses.

6. The resplendent moon-plant sacrifice, and easily digested viands, the procurers of cows, horses, and heroes, are being prepared.

7. Consecrate the sacrifice, and let the divine life-preserving, inebriating liquor go onward to Indra, and let it by our solemn rites ascend to Indra.

8. The pure, light-produced Vaiśwánara (Agni) is worshipped by many various rites, and is expanded on all sides like the heavens.

9. The pressed moon-plants are getting ready for the inebriating draught, with many songs; and the sweet liquor distils itself in a continued dripping.

10. The wise (Soma), borne up by the waves of the sea, marches along, and sustains the much-loved preparer of the sacrifice.

PRAPÁŤHAKA VI.

FIRST DAŚATI.

1. The gods come to the moon-plants procured for the sacrifice, mixed with water and the produce of the cow, after they have been bruised and properly prepared.

2. The purifying, all-beholding god goes before us in all our wars, and (the same divine fires)[1] render the Brahman glorious, through the medium of sacred rites.

3. All the pressed juices have entered the sacrificial cup; the auspicious plants are distilled. The moon-plant juice is served up ready for Indra.

4. With the speed that chariot-horses are yoked, do (our priests) bruise the pressed plants in the holy place, over the bull's hide and goat's skin.

---

[1] The addition is a plural name for Agni, to agree with the verb.

5. The wandering, radiant, ever-moving rays go forward, slaying the blackamoor Night.

6. The sacrifice-produced, inebriating moon-plant juice purifies those contaminated by destructive wars. (O Agni), send away far from us the tribe of the ungodly.

7. Do thou, accepting our offerings, purify with this aspersion of sacrificial liquid the waters in the world of human beings, as by it thou causest the Sun to shine.

8. Do thou, who suppliedst the renowned Indra with food, to enable him to slay Vritra, also purify the mighty waters.

9. O moon-plant, those drenched[1] with this thy sparkling juice, in their inebriating cups slew the (Rákshasa band, in number) ninety times nine.

10. Bring for us brilliant, enduring wealth; shed down on us provisions, with materials for sacrificial food, in this holy place.

SECOND DAŚATI.

1. The golden-coloured, far-surveying, sender down of rain,[2] the mighty one, he who is our friend, and who is famed for the loudness of his neighing, vies with the Sun in brightness.

---

[1] *Metaphorically; i. e.* had freely drunken.

[2] Indra's horse.

2. We desire this day thy presence, (O Agni,) since thou art the nimble divinity, the sucker in of our sacrificial oblations, the preserver, the greatly beloved.

3. O officiating priests, by the operation of the stones cause the juice to flow from the pressed moon-plants into the holy vessel, and purify it for the drinking of Indra.

4. That saving moon-plant by its stream of pressed sacrificial viands makes us pure. That saving moon-plant makes us pure.

5. O Soma, purify our wealth, which is counted by thousands, and maintain our heroism. Preserve also our supplies of food.

6. The ancient sages once trod the soil on which men now walk, and produced the Sun for the purpose of giving light.

7. Squeeze it out, and let the sparkling moon-plant re-echo from the receiving vessel. Sit down in the Yoni amid the liquids.

8. O Soma, rainer (down of blessings), thou art a brilliant god. O god, rainer (of blessings,) thou art served by liquid streams. O rainer (of blessings), thou acceptest the offerings we present.

9. Purify the place where our food is prepared with the streams (of sacred liquid). O Indra, descried by the intellectual among men, come hither with thy glory.

10. O Soma, rainer (of blessings), purify us with thy inebriating stream, purify the lovers of the gods, and those who love us, with thy preserving waters.

11. O mighty inebriating Soma, by this solemn rite thou art highly exalted, and bedewest (the attendant priests).

12. This all-surveying, holy, ever-moving (fire), deposited (in its receptacle with consecratory rites), carries with it aloft the powerful (moon-plant) liquid.

13. O moon-plant, thou art distilled for our benefit, that thou mayest satisfy the mighty god. It is the juice so greatly desired by the gods that sustains us, when it is produced (in abundance, so as to come) like a wave of the sea.

14. The moon-plant, with its killing spirit, slays the lovers of war for the good of the holy man, and goes to the place of preparation visited by Indra.

THIRD DAŚATI.

1. O Soma, the purifier, who, brooding over the waters, sprinklest them with thy distillations; holder of all precious things, golden fountain-god, sit down in the sacrificial Yoni.

2. Sprinkle (water, ye priests,) all around on the pressed moon-plants, which moon-plants furnish

the most excellent oblation, and which, produced for the benefit of man, has been expressed by the sacrificial stones.

3. O Soma, praised by the resounding sacrificial stones, thou art placed on the two goats' skins, like men sitting on a seat of two bulls' hides, and the horse Harí[1] enters and takes his seat among the vessels of prepared liquid.

4. O Soma, come to the feast of the gods, in which the sparkling juice overflows as the sea with the waters; for at thy distilled spirit-receiving vessel thou art inebriating yet composing.

5. The moon-plant praised in songs by the eucharistic, dripping noise of the vessels placed on the goats' skins, comes with the speed of a horse in green drippings,—comes in inebriating drippings.

6. O Soma, I and my friends praise thee. O moon-plant, daily do I and my friends praise thee. The Rákshasas are all about; save us, leave others, and come within our enclosure.[2]

7. O open-handed-prepared moon-plant, thou expandest thy voice through the ocean of juice. O purified (Soma), thou dispersest abundance of the much-desired yellow treasure.

---

[1] *i. e.* Indra's horse.

[2] The original is Parichi; *i. e.* the guardian palás-wood staff which is laid outside the sacred enclosure, and which nothing unclean must pass.

8. The wise men, the lovers of the inebriating juice, the distillers of the intoxicating moon-plant liquid, purify the inebriating spirits in the abode of man over the sacred receiving-vessel.[1]

9. O Soma, our purifier, enclosed in the vessels which rest on the two goats' skins, thou art possessed of intelligence. Do thou prepare for us a sacrifice worthy of the Rishi Angiras.

10. The pressed, inebriating moon-plant juice is being purified and strained, and, while it drips by a thousand streams, men consecrate it on the goats' skins.

11. Receiver of provisions, inebriating Soma, do thou, who at the first didst reduce the world to form for the benefit of the gods, purify us all with the liquid element.

12. The purifying, inebriating moon-plants, beloved by the Marudgana, by Indra, and by his horses, are flowing down in a continued dripping, surpassing every thing in holiness.

FOURTH DAŚATI.

1. O dripping, purifying divinity, sit down speedily among our guests, strain the strengthening liquid. The purifiers lead thee, the supplier of

[1] In the original Samudra, called usually the Drona Kalaśa.

nourishment, with cords to the place where the sacred grass is spread, as men lead a horse.

2. The orator-divinity (Soma) narrates the illustrious actions of thee as well as Śukra himself, and he, the performer of mighty acts, the brother of the pure, the purifier, the assumer of the form of a boar, marches to us on foot, singing eucharistic songs.

3. Agni, the sacrifice-attracting divinity, produced the three Vedas, the rite of sacrifice, and the Brahmanical incantations; and as the cows approach the lord of the herd, so do the inquisitive, loving intelligences approach the god Soma.

4. The god who passionately desires the sacrifice, the purifier, the golden one, and who, along with the gods, prepares the liquor and the pressed juice, the singer of eucharistic hymns, the inviter of the gods, comes to his state of purity with the eagerness the officiating priest goes to the house where there is an animal sacrifice.

5. Soma[1] is being purified; he is the father of intelligences, the father of heaven, the father of fire, the father of the Sun, the father of Indra, the father even of Vishnu.

6. The moon-plant is being sprinkled with waters

---

[1] Soma, or the moon-plant, is here personified and described as the Supreme Spirit.

copious as from the sea in the place where are the three daily sacrifices, the procurers of rain, the stay of bread, the support of multitudes,—where are the lovely voices of the chanters, and the much-desired gifts.

7. The great, overflowing, indestructible sea of moon-plant juice proceeded forth in the beginning, creating and producing all beings. It is the lord of the world, produced on the mountain-tops, and dripping near the sacred increase-causing goats' skins.

8. The purifying green-coloured moon-plant juice, uttering its own praise, rests upon the womb of its water-containing receptacle, and, drawn out by men, is prepared for our solemnities, and then brings forth native intelligence, as well as sustains bodily vigour.

9. O Indra, that sweet-flavoured moon-plant of thine, the drencher of him who drenches (the earth), is being distilled into the holy receptacle: it,—the giver of thousands as well as the giver of hundreds, the giver of manifold gifts, that is stationed on the eternal, food-providing, sacrificial grass.

10. O sweet, truth-inspiring liquid, O overshadowing Soma, be purified, thou who art produced on the mountains, and prepared over the goats' skins; do thou, most sweet, inebriating liquor, of which Indra drinks, descend into the sacred receptacle.

FIFTH DAŚATI.

1. O Agni, as the brave general, the director of the chariots of war, when he arrives distributes the riches conferred by heaven, so that his army exults with joy; in like manner does the god Soma bring for his friends robes that delight the beholders.

2. When, O holy Soma, creating thy sweet liquid streams, thou approachest the goat's skin, then, O purifying spirit, thou, by a new production, sanctifiest the place of the waters, and satisfiest the Sun with provisions by thee supplied.

3. Do ye celebrate the gods in distinguished lays. O Soma, come here to obtain a large store of wealth. Let the god Soma, who tastes sweet to holy men, sit down at the sacred receptacle of the liquid placed on the goats' skins.

4. The loving father of heaven and earth comes like a chariot, bringing provisions, and goes to Indra, making sharp the weapons of war, and holding all riches in his hands.

5. When the enlightener of the mind, the word of the Ancient One, the establisher of heaven and earth, first of all produced the illustrious venerable lord Soma, he led him to the sacred receptacle of inebriating waters.

6. When the firmly-grasping ten sisters[1] of our

[1] *i. e.* the fingers.

heroes are engaged in squeezing out the purified liquid, the green watery juice drips out on all sides from the holders of the bow, as the daughter of the Sun[1] spreads herself abroad on all sides in the sacred vessel, or as fleet horses (surround a city).

7. As among kings, or among learned men in the assembly of the sages, or among rustics, emulation is produced; so in this sacrifice, where the covered up liquid is being purified, whenever (a similar spirit prevails), I, like the Brahman armed with the sacrificial staff, sing verses to procure the increase of our cattle.

8. The nourishing moon-plant juice is being purified, the herds of cows slay the Rákshasas, and oppose the enemy. Let Soma, united with us, please Indra with his inebriating juice, and procure for us abundance of wealth, showing himself glorious amid all opposition.

9. Be sanctified, O Soma, by this purifying operation. Thou passest bravely through the water on horseback; thy speed is equal to that of the wind, and, like the Rishi Purumedha, thou savest men when they fall into sin.

10. The adorable Soma made that Mighty Essence when the womb of ocean covered up all the gods: he, the purifier, placed in Indra all his might, and the same Soma produced the solar radiance.

---

[1] *i. e.* water.

11. With the speed of a swift chariot-horse, the priest, with a fixed mind and one mental effort, prepares the sacrifice; the ten sisters purify the attractive juice, which was produced on the mountain-top, and prepared on the goats' skins in our houses.

12. Like as the waves of water follow one another, so do the guests who go to the moon-plant banquet, and come up to and enter within the venerable radiant enclosure.

SIXTH DAŚATI.

1. Prepare by beating with stones this victory-conferring viand, with the alacrity men beat a long-tongued dog.

2. This wealth and prosperity conferring, purifying Soma, the lord of all, the soul of the world, in the person of the Sun, enlightens the heaven and the earth.

3. The pressed, most pleasant, inebriating, holy moon-plants are being strained: let the spirituous liquor proceeding from them enter the gods.

4. The brilliant, pressed moon-plants, the riches of the earth, friendly and void of any hurtful quality, which are of a pleasant taste, and prepare the road to heaven, are now being got ready.

5. Distil for us the substantial viand, desired by

hundreds, and satisfying thousands ; itself valuable, and possessed of a brilliant splendour.

6. The Brahmans, void of malice, sing praises before the beloved, much-desired presence of Indra, with the affection cow-mothers lick their calves in the day they are produced.

7. As the cow exerts all her might in the much-loved action of cleaning her calf, so does the purified, carefully mixed moon-plant juice make its entrance into the presence of the sages, for the promotion of happiness and accurate judgment.

8. The priests are purifying on the goats' skins the much-desired, green-coloured Soma, which goes along with the intoxicating liquor, on every side, to all the gods.

9. This man desires food, that he may prepare a sacrifice ; and the priests celebrate the divine praise, with a voice as loud as that of a dog driven away hungry from a sacrifice.

SEVENTH DAŚATI.

1. In the presence of the beloved names (of the sacrificial adjuncts), this mighty (moon-plant juice), being placed with consecratory rites, is being purified, and rises superior to all the rest. This mighty one, the surveyor of all things, mounts the swift-going chariot of the mighty Sun.

2. Let the sounding, well-pressed moon-plant juice, which steals the affections of the mighty gods, come to us: let it be to us an invigorating, delight-inspiring, foe-destroying lord, and accept our services.

3. The pleasant juice sounds in the sacred vessel. It is like the thunderbolt of Indra, the most brilliant among brilliants. At our sacrifices the graceful, butter-yielding milch-cows let down their milk.[1]

4. The moon-plant enters into union with Indra. The friend then does not slay him who is praised by his friend, no more than a man slays a young woman. Now the moon-plant is distilling itself through the strainer into the sacred vessel.[2]

5. The supporter of the heavens, about to become a liquid, the strengthener of the gods, the intoxicator, the green fugacious herb, is not prepared in vain by holy men; it procures food and water.

6. The distiller of intellect, the brilliant moon-plant, the preserver of day, the drawer-out of the rays of the morn, sounds in the vessel of liquid juice, and enters the breast of Indra along with the wise men.

---

[1] Or the lovely, gift-conferring, water-giving rays of light distil showers of rain.

[2] *Add as understood,* 'and by its noise praising us; therefore Indra will not slay us.'

7. The seven milch-cows[1] yielded the milk of uncontaminated, mixed moon-plant juice to the three daily sacrifices, in this sacred place, and (Soma) made the four shining worlds and their appendages, which we exalt by the performance of sacrifices which tend to enlarge the understanding.

8. O Soma, let the pressed, strained, disease-destroying moon-plant juice be kept for Indra; let not the Rákshasas partake of thy enchanting juice. Let the encircling moon-plants, arranged on the two skins, be present with us.

9. The pressed, bloodless, green moon-plant, the distiller (of sweet juice), like a king in glittering array, utters his voice before the fiery coruscations; and the purifier comes like a hawk to the goats' skins, to squat himself by the liquid-containing vessel Yoni.

10. The inebriating moon-plants, placed on the sacred grass, and uttering their proper sound, are now giving out their juice before the gods, as the milch-cow does to her calf; and the radiance proceeding from the moon-plant upholds the intellect, which has been distilled from it.

11. (Agni), the preserver of gold, shines, darts his flames, surrounds the sacrifice, kindles it, and

---

[1] These are metres, rays, horses, flames of fire mothers, worlds, hells, preparations of Soma, seas, lakes, or vital airs.

licks up with his sweet tongue the swelling mighty ocean, the first of all drams in the Soma juice.

12. O lord of food, thou encirclest the holy, rich (sacrifice): the cool-bodied, diseaseless lord diffuses himself around the sacrifices, that come from all quarters; and the leafless, far-carried plants distil their essence into the sacred vessel.

EIGHTH DAŚATI.

1. These green, pressed, heaven-conducting, deposited, prepared moon-plants come into the presence of Indra, the giver of rain.

2. O wakeful Soma, go strain the moon-plant for Indra; bring the sparkling, heaven-conducting, invigorating (liquor).

3. O my friends, sit you down, and sing to obtain the favour of the purifier. Adorn him with your sacrifice, as a (mother does her) child.

4. O my friends, do ye celebrate the purifier for his inebriating quality; feed him with the rich delicious offerings, as a (mother does her) child.

5. As the calf twines itself around the life of the cow, so dost thou around the flame of the sacrifice; and all the pleasant things of which men have experience are inferior to the two-coloured Soma.[1]

---

[1] The two colours are green and yellow; the former that

6. O sweet-flavoured Soma, purify by thy might the moon-plants for the banquet of the gods with streams of liquid: sit down before our sacred vessel.

7. Soma, the purifier, sanctifies by his juice the goats' skins; and the performer of the consecratory rites utters his voice where our eucharistic hymns are sung.

8. Praise is pronounced for the sanctifier, Soma, the possessor of intelligence; since our wages fill us with wisdom to desire the performance of his worship.

9. O pressed moon-plant, possessor of herds of cows, surrounded with horses, all-powerful, the giver of gifts, assume thy pure white colour for our benefit, in the presence of the produce of the cow.

10. Do ye praise, on our account, with all the extent of your voice, your own possessor of riches. We cover thy white flame with the produce of the cow.

11. The taker away (of the sin) of the plucker up (of the Soma plant) is being purified on the goats' skins. Quickly distil wealth for the heroic descendants of the celebrators of thy praise.

---

of the plant while growing, and the latter its colour when withering.

12. The purifying Soma is being distilled at the sweet dripping vessel; praise him in the seven metres with the words of the Rishis.

NINTH DAŚATI.

1. O Soma, purify for Indra the most sweet and richly prepared spirituous liquor, the mighty, light-diffusing liquor.

2. O lord of food, increase our provisions and our mighty renown. O god, mix the mid-day bowl, beloved by the gods.

3. Praise and sprinkle on all sides, as you would do to a horse, the sacrificial moon-plant juice, which procures salvation, runs through the world, is diffused through water, and purified by mixture with other liquids.

4. That Soma, who distils spirits, who has a thousand drippings, the sprinkler, the sealer of heaven, is the possessor of all kinds of wealth.

5. I praise that Soma, who is the bringer of treasures, the bringer of riches, the bringer of food, and of brave heroes.

6. O divine (Soma), the bestower of holy future births, thou art most heavenly, and art praised for the procuring of immortality.

7. This most inebriating, pressed moon-plant dripping juice is being purified by the waters,

and is performing its frolics like the waves of the sea.

8. The bulls and cows that have strength to split even a rock, are gathering around the cow-house. O Savita, upholder of all things, give us for our portion the possession of cows and horses.

[End of the consecratory verses.]

SÁMA VEDA

SANHITÁ.

PART II.

FIRST ADHYÁYA.

1. O my heroes, sing ye before this purified moon-plant juice, which is ready to be offered up to the gods. (O Soma), the holy sages are preparing to offer up thy divinity, beloved by the gods, along with the sweet produce of the cow, to the deity (Indra). O resplendent deity, do thou distil in purity happiness for our cows, happiness for our sons, happiness for our horses, and happiness for our vegetable productions.

2. The white moon-plant juice, mixed with the produce of the cow, is distinguished by its shining radiance and ever-sounding dripping stream. The powerful (Soma), stimulated by the stimulating (songs of praise), and placed in his sacred recess, carries on the (sacrificial) conflict with the spirit of brave soldiers entering the field of battle. O all-

wise (Soma), who by thy heavenly path comest frequently to confer on us felicity, do thou, who art mighty in power, and the source of all prosperity, cause thy pure waters to drip down in our presence.

3.[1] O all-wise (divinity), source of nourishment, the streams of juice which are extracted from thy purified essence, and which are desirous of union with the sacrificial viands, flow down with the celerity of horses just broken loose from their trammels.[2] Our fingers have repeatedly manifested a desire to handle the sweet distilled juice, which is strained clear through the goats' hair strainer into the receiving-vessel. The moon-plant juice descends into the liquid-receiving ocean,[3] the womb of the genuine spirit,[4] with the alacrity that new-calved cows return to their homes.

4. O Agni, when praised, come to our banquet, to forward the offerings to the gods. Sit down, O herald, on the sacred grass. O son of Angiras, we make thee grow great by offerings of brightly-flaming clarified butter. O thou, who art ever-young, shine forth with all thy radiance. O resplendent divinity, mighty Agni, do thou confer

---

[1] To be repeated at the time of performing sacred ablutions.—*Bh.*

[2] Repeated before lifting the vessel from the ground.—*Bh.*

[3] *i. e.* the receiving-vessel.

[4] *Or* the seat of the sacrifice; the original is (Yoni).

upon us abundant, fame-procuring, ever-enduring wealth.

5. O Mitra and Varuna, performers of merit-procuring acts, abundantly refresh with showers of rain our cattles' pasture-land, and with sweet heavenly influences our appointed abode (in a future world). O performers of holy acts, praised by multitudes, extolled in many a sacred hymn by numerous melodious voices, ye rule by the greatness of your might. O ye who were praised by Jamadagni, conferrers of benefits in reward of sacrifice, sit down on the sacrificial seat (Yoni), and drink the moon-plant juice.

6. Come, O Indra, and drink the moon-plant juice, which we have pressed out for thee. Sit down on this our carpeting of sacred grass. Let thy flowing-maned draught-horses Harí, which are yoked simply by uttering an incantatory word,[1] convey thee into our presence, and do thou listen there to our sacred songs. O Indra, we Brahmans, preparers and offerers of the pressed moon-plant juice, call on thee, the drinker of the beverage, in appropriate hymns of praise.

7. O Indra and Agni, influenced by our songs, come from heaven to the splendid moon-plant banquet, and, influenced by our works,[2] drink of

---

[1] So Brahma-yujá is here explained.

[2] *Or* intellectual attainments.

the juice. O Indra and Agni, (Soma), who (for the purpose of rewarding his works) is united to the offerer of praise, who is manifested in sacrifices, and stimulates the senses, is now coming on your account. Influenced therefore by this our invitation, drink this expressed juice. By offering sacrifice, we worship Indra and Agni, who reward the celebrators of their praise. Let them satiate themselves with this our moon-plant beverage.

8. The origin of thy juice, (O Soma,) is from above; and thy vast stocks of exhilarations and nourishment, though having their seat in heaven, are yet appropriated by the inhabitants of earth. O purifier of those who acquire riches, do thou drench with thy juice our Indra and Varuna along with the Maruts. Desirous of procuring thy favour, we worship thee; for all the requisite materials for sacrifices proceed from thee.

9. O Soma, after brooding over the waters, and being purified by distillation, thou flowest down. O holder of all valuable treasures, golden divinity, everlasting fountain of waters, thou sittest down on the holy sacrificial Yoni. The divine, exhilarating, delight-inspiring, primeval udder, Soma, the purifier, has his seat in the firmament. (O divine Spirit), thou art worthy to be called down, and taken hold of; for when thoroughly washed by the hands of our priests, thou, the beholder of all

things, distillest thyself as the imparter of nourishment.

10. O Soma, sit down quickly on the receiving-vessel, and, purified by the priests, distil thyself in the place where the sacrificial viands are deposited. The men whose duty it is to cleanse thee, lead thee with their rope-shaped fingers to the washing, in the place where the sacred grass is strewed, as they would a powerful horse. The god Soma, who is arrayed in splendid armour, and is the slayer of the Rákshasas, is now being purified. He saves from all misfortune, is the protecting father of the gods, possessed of surpassing might, the supporter of heaven, and upholder of earth. The far-seeing, wise, precedence-receiving Ushaná, greatly distinguished among men by his poetic lays, obtained the concealed milk, treasured up in these beauteous cows.[1]

11. O valiant Indra, with the affection that newly-calved cows low for their calves, do we offer up praises to thee, the omniscient god, the ruler of all animate, and lord of all inanimate creatures. O celestial Indra, there is no one to be compared with thee either in heaven or in earth, none who

---

[1] Probably the meaning is, that he was the first to extract the moon-plant juice from the plants, and produce by means of it a fermented liquor.

existed in times past, and none who shall exist in times to come. Therefore we, who anxiously desire horses, cows, and provisions, call on thee.

12. With what oblation, or with what solemn rite, performed with the utmost sacred science, will the ever-increasing, glorious, friendly Indra be moved to favour us with his presence? Let (Soma), who among the producers of inebriety is ever faithful, and who among sacrificial viands is to be chiefly esteemed, break open[1] for thee (O Indra) the well-secured treasures (of our foes). O Indra, preserver of our friends who celebrate thy praise, thou art ever present for our protection in a hundred ways.

13.[2] (O priests), we praise all the day long that renowned, foe-destroying Indra of yours, who gets muzzy on the sacrificial beverage placed in the sacred vessels, with voices raised as loud as those of milch-cows lowing for their calves. (Indra), we desire of thee quickly to give us food of heavenly origin, worthy of being bestowed, encircled with majesty as a mountain with clouds, capable of feeding multitudes, worthy of being extolled in hundreds and thousands of different kinds of measure, and, united with it, abundance of cows.

---

[1] Imperative, on the authority of the Bh.

[2] By Vadha Rishi, in praise of Indra.

14. O ye oppressed priests, who sing the long verses of the Sáma during the moon-plant banquet, in praise of Indra, who knows the place of riches, and who, to afford you protection, comes with his swift horses, I too call upon him in this sacrifice, as (a dependent calls on) the supporter of the family to perform what he desires. Neither demons, nor gods, nor men can overcome Indra of graceful countenance, who, when he has reverently received the exhilarating beverage with the sacrificial food, confers distinguishing wealth on the sacrificer, who extols him, and celebrates his praise.

15. (O Soma), send down pure, in thy exhilarating distillation, the moon-plant juice for Indra's drinking. Soma, the slayer of the Rákshasas, the beholder of all things, delights to sit on the Yoni, beat upon by the fingers with gold rings, where also the receiving-vessel is placed.[2] O thou richest possessor of wealth, do thou become a bountiful bestower, a most zealous slayer of foes, and a transferrer of the wealth of the rich among them to us.

16. O Soma, thou art most pleasant to the taste, the ever-ready prosperer of our rites, the causer of exhilaration, the mighty one, the all-brilliant

---

[1] *Or* where (the juice-expressers) are seated on their buttocks. The Brahmans who perform these ceremonies must all wear a kind of flattened gold ring.

inebriator; do thou then strain out thy juice pure for Indra. When we have drunk of thee, then the rainer of blessings rains them in abundance. When we have drunk of thee, then the beholder of all things, the god who surpasses all in intellect, eagerly seizes and bears to us the stored-up provisions (of our foes), like a war-horse rushing into the battle.

17. Let these pressed, quickly prepared, green, all-surveying draughts of moon-plant juice find an entrance into the presence of Indra, the rainer of blessings. This expressed moon-plant juice, necessary to be adored for our protection in war, is being purified for Indra. Soma knows that all-conquering Indra as intimately as he is known (by any intelligence). When in his cups, Indra seizes his adorable, easily handled bow, and he who warred against the celestial serpent[1] lays hold of his rain-dispensing thunderbolt.

18. O my friends, drive away the long-tongued dog of a demon, who would approach the ever-victory-conferring sacrificial viands placed beside the exhilarating expressed juice. The moon-plant juice, which in purifying streams distils itself with the speed of a horse, is now about to be prepared. Let my heroes address themselves with a ready

---

[1] *Or* against Vritra, to obtain water.

mind to all the rites needful for the sacrifice of the indestructible Soma.

19. The consecrated food is being purified in the presence of the delight-inspiring, adorable liquids, and the all-powerful Soma is growing great among the waters of heaven; and that mighty god who surveys all things, has mounted the every-where-going chariot of the mighty Sun. The tongue of the sacrifice, the orator, the protector of this solemn rite, the indestructible (Soma), purifies the exhilarating, pleasant juice. The son now takes his third name,[1] which his parents did not recognise, but by which he becomes illustrious in heaven. The shining juice sounds over the sacred vessel, and is confined by men in the yellow-tinged receiver. The strainers of the juice for this solemnity raise their voices, where thou, Soma, shinest at the morning sacrifice.

20. With sacrifice after sacrifice, and hymn after hymn, do we extol Agni, who confers upon us prosperity. We highly praise him, who is immortal, the parent of wealth, and beloved even as a friend. We praise him, the offspring of the sacrificial oblations; for he loves us. We present our offerings to him who forwards our oblations to the gods. Let

---

[1] This third name is Somayájí. The first is his own proper name; the second is that of the constellation under which he was born; to these is now superadded his priestly name, with the giving of which his parents have no right to interfere.

him be our protector in war, our prosperer, and the preserver of our children.

21. Come, O Agni, listen to the divine hymns of praise which I, in sincerity, harmoniously utter before thee. Grow great by this our moon-plant oblation. Wherever thy spirit is, there thou layest hold of the excellent, strength-producing offering, and there thou preparest a place for the production of the sacred juice. Be thou the preserver of the most unskilful among the performers of sacrifice, that they fall not into the sin of destroying thy radiance; and accept thou of their services.

22. O grasper of the thunderbolt, we, the offerers of the sacred viands, and desirous of preservation, call on thee, manifested anew in this sacrifice, as men do on some mighty hero. O performer of sacred rites for our preservation, Indra, ever-young and terrible, seizer (of the enemy), may we through thee be rendered secure. We, thy friends, worship thee, the lord, the preserver, the adorable divinity.

23. O thou, who art celebrated in hymns of praise, we approach thee at the present time for all the adorable things we wish, with the vivacity travellers exhibit in laving water on their fellows. O hero, grasper of the thunderbolt, as seas are fed by rivers, so do our praises daily magnify thee. The celebrators of praise offer oblations to the two

mighty horses Harí, belonging to the fast-travelling (Indra), which are joined by an incantatory word to the large yoke of the chariot, are the conveyers of Indra (to us), and are acquainted with the roads of heaven.

[End of the first Adhyáya.]

SECOND ADHYÁYA.

1. Praise ye Indra, the drinker of the juice offered in sacrifices, the sustainer of all things, the performer of merit-conferring works, the bestower of riches on men.[1] Speak the praises of Indra, sacrificed to by multitudes, praised by myriads, worthy to be celebrated in songs, famed through eternal ages. Indra is indeed the bestower of rich supplies, the mover of all things,[2] the mighty one, who brings into our possession all that is valuable.

2. O my friends, do ye sing to the moon-plant-juice-drinking Indra, who possesses the two horses Harí, a delight-inspiring song. Let our other heroes sing a splendid hymn to the conferrer of splendid gifts, the giver of real wealth. O Indra, give us food equal to our desires; performer of many merit-conferring works, give us cattle equal to our de-

---

[1] *Or* reverenced by men. [2] *Or* bringer of all things.

sires; and give gold equal to our desires; for it is thou that appointest our place of abode.

3. We, thy friends, who desire thy favour, praise thee for that purpose in sacred hymns, as the sons of Kanwa were wont to do. O holder of the thunderbolt, we praise thee, and no other, in this new sacrifice, attended with various rites; and thee we also acknowledge in our praises. The gods love the institutor of sacrifices; they never allow him to become a driveller; they go quickly to his exhilarating beverage.

4. Let our songs of praise celebrate on every side the juice expressed for the exhilaration of Indra; and let the singers of the hymns extol the venerable Soma. We invite to this expressed juice that Indra in whom all glory especially resides, and whom the seven priests[1] delight. For whom the gods prepare the wisdom-giving rites in the Trikadraka sacrifice, that Indra our voices extol.

5. O Indra, the purified moon-plant juice placed on the sacred grass is for thee; come quickly, and drink it. O sender down of rays, this conspicuous, adorable, expressed juice delights thee. Destroyer of foes, thou art especially invited. O Shringa, offspring of Vrisha,[2] the liquor which sustains thee,

[1] See Preface.

[2] Vrisha was a Rishi sprung from Indra's water; *or translate* 'Shringa, offspring of the Sun.'

when quaffed from the vessels, is that on which the mind especially rests.

6. O Indra, thou art possessed of a large hand; therefore do thou with thy right hand for us lay hold on accumulated riches, such as are worthy of being praised, and worthy of our acceptance. We know thee as the performer of many religious rites, the liberal giver, the wealthy, the most adorable, the god who is accompanied with an all-protective force. Neither god nor man can attempt to oppose thee, more than one would a formidable bull.

7. O sender down of rain, we prepare by pressure expressed moon-plant juice for thy drinking. Partake of the satisfying exhilarating beverage. Do not slay ignorant men who desire thee to save them, nor render them objects of contempt; and do not respect those who hate the Brahmans. Let the moon-plant juice prepared in our sacrifice, along with the produce of the cow, delight thee, so as to procure for us great riches. Drink of it as the deer does of the water of the lake.

8. O Indra, who givest us a place of abode, drink to thy satisfaction of our expressed nourishing (liquor). O thou who art insusceptible of fear from any quarter, we present it to thee. The expressed juice, washed by the priests, and purified by the stones and goats' hair, becomes clean as a horse washed in the river. We, by mixing the barley-

offering with the produce of the cow, prepare the delicious beverage. Indra, we invite thee to the feast which has the accompaniment of the exhilarating liquor.

9. O lord of riches, this juice, expressed by the might of our priests, is served up in proper order. O recipient of praise, drink thou of it. Introduce thy body into the sacrificial viands which Soma is preparing for thee. O drinker of the moon-plant juice, let it produce in thee its exhilarating effects. Let the moon-plant juice fill thy two sides. Let the juice, accompanied with songs, diffuse itself through thy body, and then come to us with both thy arms laden with riches.

10. O my friends, ye offerers up of praise, come quickly, and sit down, and sing the praises of Indra. During the performance of the pressed moon-plant sacrifice, do ye, in one body,[1] (celebrate) Indra, the slayer of hosts of foes, and the possessor of much valuable wealth. Let him be present with us, through union to himself, in wealth, and in the bestowal of an enlarged understanding.[2] Let him, without fail, come to us in all kinds of food.

11. O my friends, in re-union after re-union, and conflict after conflict, in the performance of sacrifice, do we call upon the powerful Indra for protection.

---

[1] *Or* in alternate bands.

[2] *Or* wives.

I call on him in regular order, who comes from his ancient abode to be present at many a sacrifice,—on him on whom my father in ancient times called. When he hears to-day our invitation, let him come with a thousand auxiliaries, and with stores of food.

12. Thou, O Indra, in this moon-plant sacrifice purifiest the offerer of oblations, and the celebrator of thy praise, for the obtaining of still increasing strength; for thou art the mighty one. He is the extoller of the sacrificer in the highest heaven, and also in the assembly of the gods; he carries him through every difficulty, he supplies him abundantly with food, he is the conqueror of the aerial (Rákshasas) powers. I call on the mighty Indra to give us food, and for aid in this engagement.[1] Let him be very near us in the singing of sacred hymns, and, as a friend, promote our prosperity.

13. By this hymn I invite Agni, the giver of strength, the beloved, the intelligent, the attendant at sacrifices, who is manifested in propitious rites, the inviter to every sacred ceremony, the immortal. Let him yoke[2] his all-protecting red horses, and, when invoked, let him hasten to bring the gods. He is the recipient of praise, (the god) to whom

---

[1] It may be in war, or in sacrifice; the word means both.

[2] Or accompanied by, &c., radiance.

sacrifice is offered, and is the performer of meritorious acts; therefore the wealth of the inhabitants of the world is offered to this resplendent divinity.

14. The gloom-dispelling (morn), daughter of heaven, appears, and, becoming mighty, with her brilliant eye dissipates the darkness, and the bearer of blessings ushers in the light. The Sun, uniting with her rays, advances and beautifies all the constellations that bespangle the heavens. Mean while, aided by the solar and lunar light, we assemble along with our sacrificial viands.

15. O radiant sons of Aświni, these heaven-desiring oblations call on you. I too call on (all) the possessors of merit united to wealth. Do ye then go to every individual among them. Do ye, O heroes, lay hold of collected heaps of provisions, and send them to the singers of your praise. Stop your chariot at our door, and drink the sweet moon-plant liquor.

16. The Brahmans are milking out the resplendent white milk, which forms the primeval, manifold-gift-conferring, all-surveying body of this moon-plant sacrifice. This (Soma), like the Sun, the surveyor of all things, runs into the thirty vessels[1] at the mid-day sacrifice, and, like the seven rivers,

---

[1] *Or* for thirty days; in allusion to the thirty Ghatikas in a day.

has his source in the heavens. As the Divine Sun, so this Soma is placed above all worlds.

17. This gold-coloured, brilliant, moon-plant juice, produced for the service of the gods by a primeval birth, is now being distilled in the holy place. This brilliant (divinity), accompanied by the intellectual hymn; this sage, united to the institutor of this sacrifice, is carrying on this rite to its consummation, for the benefit of the gods. O Soma, wherever in a holy place thy primeval juice is being milked out and distilled, there thou art born anew in the presence of the gods.

18. O purifier, bring our friends near us, and inspire our enemies with fear; confer on us their wealth. The gods are come to the newly-produced, foe-destroying, liquid moon-plant juice. Sing hymns of praises before it, O my heroes.

19. The intellect-sharpening streams of moon-plant juice repair to the receiving waters, as the mighty stags do to the forests. The ash-coloured, shining juice flows forward in a stream for the sacrifice, procuring for us food and herds of cows. Let the pressed moon-plant juice flow out for Indra, Váyu, the Maruts, and Vishnu.

20. O brilliant Soma, by means of pure water thou art rendered drinkable at the banquet of the gods, as the sea also is drunk (in the form of pure water). And now, inebriating and ever-wakeful

(Soma), in the form of the juice of the divided plant, thou wendest thy way to the vessel that receives the sweet distilled liquid. The much-desired (Soma), loved as a son, white, and sprinkled with water, shows himself to advantage by his varied movements, and (the fingers) of the two arms send him into the resounding waters, with the swiftness that the fleet warriors urge their chariots (into the field of battle).

21. The moon-plants, distillers of sweet juice, pressed during the sacrifice, proceed onward to procure food [1] for our officiating priests. Truly as one of the number enters a flock of geese, so does (Soma) enter the minds of all (his worshippers); when, as a horse is, he has been sprinkled with water. Of a truth the fingers of Trita Rishi cause the green moon-plants to flow down in juice, for the drinking of Indra, by means of the bruising-stones.

22. With this stream, O Soma, thou who desirest the presence of the gods, drop down to where sounding throughout the holy place thou movest on all sides. The much-desired stream of juice is being produced, the gold-coloured Soma is being purified; [and with celerity cleanses the unrighteous, and distils for the singers of praise

---

[1] *Or* fame.

the fame which is procured by a band of heroes.] Of the nourishing sacrificial liquids [let no marrer of sacred rites hear even the sound. Drive away therefore every dog, as polluting the solemnity, in the manner the sons of Bhrigu beat off the dog Makka].[1]

[End of the second Adhyáya.]

THIRD ADHYÁYA.

1. O Soma, do thou, who holdest the first place among the gods, purify our sons with all thy varied aids, and in an especial degree also all our sacred hymns. O beholder of all things, first among the gods, when thou hast made our hymns of praise to ascend, cause showers of rain to distil themselves from heaven. O thou, who presidest over every religious rite, all the worlds exist for thy glory, and for thee the cows run (to the milking-pail).

2. O pressed Soma, rainer of blessings, distil thyself, make us illustrious in the earth, and slay all that hate us. O Soma, filled with this thy excellent, nourishing juice, by thy aid we shall subdue all our foes. By these thy dreaded sharp

---

[1] The two passages enclosed in brackets are apparently a late addition, as wanting in the best MSS., and marked as doubtful in the Bháshya. If omitted, the line between them must begin with 'for,' instead of 'of.'

weapons, made to slay our foes, do thou save us from all that hate us.

3. O Soma, rainer of blessings, thou art glorious; O rainer of blessings, brilliant deity, thou art the producer of rain; O rainer of blessings, thou art the support of religious rites. O rainer of blessings, thy might causes rain, thy worship causes rain, thy juice causes rain; and, O rainer of blessings, thy person causes rain. Thou, O rainer of blessings, makest a noise like that of a horse. O Soma, send us cows, send us horses; open to us the door of wealth.

4. O purifying Soma, thou art the rainer of blessings; therefore we invoke thee, who art all-seeing and all-glorious through thy innate radiance. When thou art sprinkled with water, and purified by mortals, and received into the sacred vessel, thou (with thy flavour) fillest the whole hall of assembly. O Soma, who marchest arrayed in thy own armour, come here without fail, and, exhibiting thyself pleased, strain out pure for us a valiant progeny.

5. We earnestly desire the friendship of thee, who distillest thyself in purity, and moistenest the receiving sacred vessel. Thy waves bedew with their current the holy vessel: with these, O Soma, do thou gladden us. O purifying Soma,

lord of the universe, do thou bring for us wealth and food, along with a brave progeny.

6. We adore Agni, the herald and inviter of the gods, who is possessed of all wealth,[1] who works gloriously in the sacrifice. The men who are continually singing hymns, ever invoke in their sacred verses Agni by one name or other, as the lord of men, the bearer away of the sacrifice, and beloved by the heavenly hosts. O Agni, who art produced by the friction of two pieces of inflammable wood, bring the gods here to (the priests seated on) the holy cut grass; for thou art the inviter of the gods for us, and worthy of all our praises.

7. We call upon you to the banquet of moon-plant juice, Mitra and Varuna, who are manifested in our presence, full of holy might. I invoke Mitra and Varuna, who by their faithful word are the prosperers of holy rites, and the lords of pure light. Let Varuna be our preserver along with Mitra, and be with us for all kinds of protection; let them bestow on us all valuable kinds of riches.

8. The singers praise Indra in the hymns of the Sáma Veda; the chanters praise him in those of the Rich, and the priests of the Yajush praise him with their voices. Indra is ever accompanied by his two horses, which are yoked by the bare word of com-

---

[1] *Or* wisdom.

mand. Indra is armed with a thunderbolt,[1] and is covered with golden ornaments. O invincible Indra, be present with us, with thy mighty aids, in every skirmish, and in every war. Indra, to give light for ever, caused the Sun to ascend to heaven, and with his rays to irradiate the mountainous world.

9. We forward the increase-causing sacrificial food and well-finished eucharistic hymns to Indra and Agni; and, along with the oblation, songs that yield the milk of praise. Multitudes of wise men praise them after this manner, to obtain protection; and those who are engaged in wars do so to obtain food. We, who are the utterers of praise, the bearers of the sacred viands, and desirous of wealth, invoke with our voices you two, who are the recipients of sacrificial offerings.

10. O rainer of blessings, arrive in thy pure stream (at the receiving-vessel); be the cause of exhilaration to Indra, the companion of the Maruts, and the giver by thy might to us of all valuable things. O thou, who art the purifier, we cause thee, the sustainer of heaven and earth, the all-seeing, the powerful, to enter our sacrificial viands.[2]

---

[1] The Vajra, here translated *thunderbolt*, is a club with a round head armed with spikes.

[2] *Or* to accompany us in our wars.

Having laid hold of the green moon-plant with those your fingers, send it down in a holy stream, and send our friend into the wars.[1]

11. As a red bull lows at the sight of cows, so dost thou approach both earth and heaven; and as Indra's voice is heard in the wars, so, bestowing wisdom, thou comest to the place where the voice of the dripping is heard. O delicious Soma, that art drunk with the produce of the cow, when thou minglest thyself with the sweet juice thou sendest forth thy voice, and when sprinkled as the author of purity, thou causest a continued stream to flow for Indra. O Soma, the inebriator, do thou strain out pure, into this vessel, for our delight, the water-holding cloud, making the distiller of rain from the cloud-piercing stroke of Indra bend over us. And, O Soma, when sprinkled, do thou assume thy white colour, and, desiring the produce of our cows, pour in on us from all sides.

12. We, the celebrators of thy praise, call upon thee, that we may receive food. Our (infantry) heroes call on thee, O Indra, the preserver of holy men, when surrounded by our enemies; and those who are at the cavalry station call on thee. O venerable Indra, who holdest the thunderbolt in thy hand, and assumest the form of lightning, thou art

---

[1] *Or* into our sacrificial viands.

the mighty one, the sustainer of the universe, he who is praised by us. Give us, O Indra, cows, and horses fit for chariots, with the liberality thou givest all kinds of food to the victorious.

13. Do ye, with all these excellent sacrificial viands, since he is known to be a friend of mine, serve Indra, who is encompassed by all valuable things,[1] gives valuable jewels in thousands, and is bountiful to those that celebrate his praise. As a powerful man goes against a hundred enemies, so does Indra go to slay the enemies of the man who performs sacrifice; and the gifts of the giver of supplies of food flow in as waters collecting from the mountains.

14. O holder of the thunderbolt, this very day the heroes who fill the sacred vessel supply thee with liquor. O Indra, listen to me the offerer of praise, and come here to my home. O handsome-faced Indra, possessor of the two horses Harí, who art the recipient of praise, and greatly celebrated, we desire thy presence when in thy cups thou art adorned with thy wealth, and when at the moon-plant banquet thou art surrounded with stores of provisions, of a magnitude to become a proverb.

15. O Soma, thy juice is pleasing to the gods; it is the slayer of Rákshasas, is exhilarating, super-

---

[1] *Or* dwells in many places.

lative, and worthy of becoming nourishment to all men. Do thou purely distil thy essence. Thou didst slay the hostile Vritra, and daily art thou worshipped in the field of battle. Thou also art the bestower of cows and horses. Mixed with the produce of the cow, which is accompanied by our eucharistic hymns, do thou sit down, like a hawk, on the Yoni,[1] and display thy brilliance.

16. This adorable Soma, the nourisher, the conferrer of wealth, when purified, drips down. He is the lord of all creatures, and enlightens the two worlds. The beloved, emulous voices praise thee, to obtain thy exhilarating beverage; and the moon-plant juice, when purified and shining, prepares the road (to the object of our desire). Bring that glorious purified juice, whose sound delights the ear, by which we ask wealth for the five tribes of men.

17. Soma, the all-observing, the rainer of blessings on the possessors of wisdom, is now being purified. He who maintains the succession of the days, of the dawnings, and of the solar movements, who moves on the face of the dripping waters, is now causing his voice to be heard in the receiving-vessel, and entering the breast of Indra along with our hymns of praise. By our wise men is purified

---

[1] Yoni means *a womb*. It is in the Bháshya sometimes rendered *a seat*. It means, I infer, either the place where the alcoholic essence is generated, or where the juice is expressed.

the ancient, the wise (Soma), who, when pressed by the priests, drips down on all sides into the receiving-vessel, producing and distilling the sacred, sweet liquor, which makes the wind to blow, and procures the friendship of Indra, lord of the three worlds. The inebriating Soma, when purified, sparkles at the dawn; and he who receives increase from the liquid streams, becomes the sustainer of the world. He, when he has (by the priests) milked the twenty-one (cows), distils the milk beautiful to behold, and fitted to enter the breast of Indra.

18. O Indra, since thou undoubtedly art heroic, powerful, and unflinching, thy intellectual qualities are to be adored by all. O possessor of manifold riches, let wealth be possessed by him who (by sacrifice) sustains the gods; and afterwards, O Indra, favour us with thy society. O lord of food, who enjoyest perfect ease, who resemblest a Brahman,[1] show thyself always kind to us, by delighting thyself in drinking our expressed moon-plant juice, mixed with the produce of the cow.

19. All our songs of praise fall in showers on Indra, who fills the firmament,[2] the most expert of charioteers, the lord of provisions, and protector of holy men. O Indra, lord of strength, let not the

---

[1] *i. e.* one intent on the service of the deity.

[2] *Or* the sea.

offerers of sacred food to obtain thy friendship be afraid. We especially adore thee, the victorious and invincible. The many former gifts of Indra, and the protection he affords us, are not despised by us, when our host confers wealth, with food-supplying cows, on the singers of eucharistic hymns.

FOURTH ADHYÁYA.

1. These drops of moon-plant juice obliquely moving to their purified state,[1] and quickly giving birth to all desirable things, are being prepared for use. These powerful moon-plants destroy many sins, and procure for our sons valuable presents, and for ourselves troops of cavalry. They produce riches and cows and food for gifts to us, and run to listen to our eucharistic hymns.

2. The resplendent Soma, the purifier, during the sacrifices performed by men, marches through the air, accompanied by the hymns of the wise. O Soma, who art famed for supplying food for the gods, do thou bring for us that strength which is united with quickness of movement, and a form which shall confer on us dignity. O thou, who shinest brightly, bring to us for our protection the riches of hundreds of cows, stores of provisions,

[1] *i. e.* moving through the goat's-hair strainer.

troops of noble horses, and wealth to make us respected.

3. To enable us to perform properly our sacred rites, we supplicate thee, who dwellest in the regions of the mighty heaven, art possessed of all riches, and ever auspicious; the cutter in pieces of the powerful, the highly extolled, the performer of mighty works, the inebriator, the destroyer of hundreds of cities. O performer of merit-conferring works, let the hawk bring to thee from these heavens all dazzling and imperishable wealth. Afterwards, putting into it thy spirit, rise to superior might, O thou bestower of the object of our desire, and observer of all men. And let the bird bring without fail the sender of rain, the guardian of sacrifice, who has been ordained for the common benefit of all the gods.

4. O Soma, when purified by the wise priests, sanctify our food by thy drippings, and, bringing health-conferring provisions, come to our cows. O much-praised, white-coloured Soma, when in the course of preparation thou art strained forth pure, and goest to mingle with the produce of the cow, do thou prepare wealth and food for the people. Shining beside the sacrificial viands, do thou who art ordained for the benefit of mankind, and purified for the banquet of the gods, come to the place prepared for Indra. (The household) Agni, joined

with (the oblation-receiving) Agni, the wise, the preserver of families, the ever-young, the drawer in of the sacrifice, the spoon-mouthed, shines forth. O divine Agni, the institutor of the sacrifice worships thee, the herald of the gods: do thou prove his especial protector. Whatever institutor of a sacrifice sits down in the presence of Agni to prepare the banquet of the gods, do thou, our purifier, confer on him happiness.

5. I invoke Mitra, possessed of holy might, and Varuna, the destroyer of our foes; for they two furnish a supply of water by the act of raining. Bringing without fail the rewards of the sacrifice, O Mitra and Varuna, the increasers of water,[1] the senders down of rain, you diffuse yourselves throughout the sacrifice, complete in all its parts.

6. Mitra and Varuna are sages produced for the benefit of mankind; they have a wide place of abode; they also increase our strength, and further our sacred rites.

7. The bands of Maruts, advancing with the fearless Indra, burst upon our view. Both he and they exult with joy, and are arrayed in equal splendour. They, year by year, without fail, impregnating the clouds, send us rain, and have obtained the title of worthy of a share in the sacrifice. With the

---

[1] *Or* truth; *or* sacrifice.

breaking, tearing Maruts, thou, O Indra, didst enter the stronghold, and bring forth the cows which had been shut up in the cave.[1]

8. O Indra and Agni, I supplicate you; for by you this whole world was formed, according to the hymns of the sages: you will not destroy me your worshipper. Fierce, and the annihilators of our foes, O Indra and Agni, we invoke you; do ye have pity upon us in our present difficulty. O preserver of holy men, through means of the virtuous performers of sacrifice, slay our foes, slay the slaves that rise against us, utterly slay all that hate us.

9. The flowing drops of moon-plant juice distil in purity their inebriating, delight-inspiring essence: and with these the exhilarating juices that distil delight, and brighten up the understanding, flow down above the receiving-vessel in the holy place. The purifier, the shining, the resplendent (Soma), the grand reality, is sent with speed in a stream into the receiving-vessel; and the grand reality goes to lay hold on Mitra and Varuna. He who is pressed by men, is the object of desire, the all-seeing, the resplendent king, produced in the heavens, is being prepared.

---

[1] The cows of the gods were stolen by the Paṅi (merchant) Asurs, and rescued by Indra. The whole story is evidently the same as that of the Grecian Hercules. See Rich VII. Anuváka, 3rd Súkta.

10. The drawer together of materials for the sacrifice causes the hymns of the three Vedas to be sung, the hymns that sustain the sacrificial rites, which disclose the qualities of the all-pervading god.[1] And as cows when called repair to the master of the herd, so do the minds, that desire happiness, to Soma. The milch-cows are desirous of the moon-plants; the Brahmans by their learned hymns ask the moon-plant juice. The pressed moon-plant juice is being distilled and strained, and our Trishtup verses mingle with the moon-plant juice. O Soma, who art sprinkled and purified in these vessels, do thou purely distil for us happiness and peace. Enter thou into Indra with thy exhilarating might, increase the glory of the holy word, and produce in us enlargement of intellect.

11. O Indra, though there were a hundred heavens, they would not emit a brilliance like thine, nor could a hundred earths, no, nor even a thousand suns, nor the whole of the creatures in the two worlds, (emit), O holder of the thunderbolt, (a brilliance equal to thine). O rainer down of blessings, all-powerful Indra, thou suppliest us with every heaven-descended faculty in vast abundance. O possessor of riches, and holder of the thunderbolt, save us by thy mighty aids, while defending our cow-pens.

---

[1] *Or* Brahme.

12. O slayer of Vritra, we flow together like the drops of pressed moon-plant juice, where they drop down in the holy place, while the chanters, seated all around on the cut sacrificial grass, wait on thee. O fixer of our place of abode, the singers celebrate thee when thou minglest with the moon-plant juice. Whenever thou thirstest for moon-plant juice, come to this place, and listen, when approaching, to our beseeching cry, emitted with the constancy of perpetually sounding beings. O sustainer of all things, thou givest to the descendants of Kańwa a thousand portions of nourishing food. O giver of riches, surveyor of the universe, at present we desire of thee sustenance in the form of gold and cows.

13. He who actively engages in hymns of praise obtains food, in union with an enlarged understanding. I praise with my voice your much-extolled Indra, with the eagerness the carpenter bends the pliant metal ring round the wheel.[1] The careless chanter is not extolled among the givers of riches, nor do riches flow in on the impious neglecters of the praises of the rich; but, O possessor of riches, wealth is given to me, who on lucky days sing the hymns with gracefulness.

14. The priests utter the hymns of the three Vedas

---

[1] There is a play on the word 'nema,' which means *bend*, and *praise*.

with the affection milch-cows call upon their calves, and the drops of moon-plant juice proceed downwards with a resounding noise. The Brahmanical, mighty, sacrifice-accompanying hymns celebrate Soma, the child of heaven. O Soma, cause to flow in to us the wealth of the four seas, and also thousands of treasures from every side.

15. O Soma, the pleasant, sweet, exhilarating moon-plant juice is being purified, and drips down. Let your exhilarating juice enter the gods. The Brahman gods have said that Indu (the moon-plant juice) is distilled for Indra. (Soma), the lord of speech, the lord of all might, is being worshipped. Soma, the possessor of a thousand streams which flow together, the inspirer of the sacred songs, the lord of rich men, the friend of Indra, is being distilled to-day.

16. (O Soma), lord of incantations, thy holy essence is every where shed abroad. O author of being, thou encompassest every member of our body all around. The men devoid of fervour, and imperfectly instructed[1] in religious things, cannot embrace thy essence; but the sacrificers, who are like thoroughly baked bread, do embrace it. O Soma, burner up of our foes, thy essence is spread over the heavenly region, and its shining parts

---

[1] *Literally*, raw.

stand forth separately to view, and, quickly moving, preserve its purifier, and ascend within the heavens by their radiance. The most illustrious (Soma), in the person of the morning Sun, shines forth; and, desirous of sacrificial viands, the sprinkler of water showers it down on the earth. It was through his wisdom that the wisdom-possessing gods performed the act of creation, and the men-surveying patriarchs established the race of man.

17. O ye chanters, do ye sing to Agni, the giver of gifts, the attendant on sacrifices, the mighty one, who is possessed of a pure radiance. Agni, the wealthy, the possessor of brilliance, the recipient of sacrifices, bestows fame-procuring provisions in union with progeny. Let the amiable mind of a god like him, worthy of our society, come into our presence with supplies of food and abundance of water.

18. Indra, holder of the thunderbolt, we laud that joy-producing juice of thine, the causer of rain, the subduer of armies, the former of worlds, and which is adored by thy gold-coloured horses; by which also thou didst extend thy light to Manu, the son of Urvaśí, and, rejoicing in this sacrifice, displayest thy radiance. The singers, as on former occasions, celebrate in alternate lays that essence of thine. Do thou subdue, day by day, the waters, which are the sources of rain.

19. O Indra, hear the invocations of Toraśchi,

who performs thy solemn service. Satisfy him with the treasure of a valiant progeny, and abundance of cows; for thou art magnanimous. To him who produces the new exhilarating song, do thou impart an all-sagacious understanding, of the true ancient stamp, and continually increasing. We praise that Indra, whom our voices and the sacred hymns extol; and, desirous of worshipping his great might, we fall down in adoration before him.

[End of the fourth Adhyáya.]

FIFTH ADHYÁYA.

1. O purifying Soma, the all-pervading, beloved, heaven-descended, milky streams of juice are being produced over the receiving-vessel; and the creative priests purify thee, so that thy large drops fall down through mid-air, O thou who art the portion of the Rishis. The life-preserving streams of the unchangeable purifier proceed in all directions to both the worlds, when the green plant is purified in the holy place, and sit on the receiving-vessel over the spirit-generating womb. O beholder of all things, the mighty beams of thee, the ever-increasing, proceed on all sides to the universal mansion, (the bodies of the gods); whilst thou, O all-pervading Soma, art in thy indestructible juice poured forth pure, and reignest supreme over every land.

2. The purifier, sprung from heaven, all-wondrous like a flash of lightning, appears in a mighty flame called Vaiśwánara (the friend of all men). O brilliant purifier, the Rákshasa-dispelling, inebriating essence of thy juice is flowing down purified through the goat's-hair strainer. The happiness-conferring, shining juice of thee, our purifier, displays its splendour; and thou, the seer of all things, spreadest thy light all abroad.

3. As cows cheerfully go (to the cow-house), so do these quick-moving, shining, ever-advancing moon-plants, stript of their black skins, (go to their place). We praise the Rákshasa-restraining, difficultly-obtained, enduring, inebriation-generating, bark-divested stalks of the present excellent moon-plants. The voice of the mighty purifier is heard descending like a shower of rain, and his rays shine in the heavens. O Soma, strain out pure for us abundance of food, joined with abundance of cows, of gold, of horses, and heroic sons. Do thou, O beholder of all things, distil out pure for us thy juice, and satisfy the two extended worlds, as the Sun by his rays distils the morning. O Soma, do thou with thy golden streams encompass us on all sides, as the earth is encompassed on all sides with water.

4. O Soma, possessed of an exalted mind, having assumed thy body, beloved by the gods, go on all

sides, saying, "(I go) wherever the gods are." Consecrating the unconsecrated, and providing food for the people, send down showers of rain from heaven. He who moves with speed to the highest heavens, distils floods of water while seated in the holy place. When pressed, thou comest quickly into thy holy state, accompanied with thy might, possessed of radiance, seeing all things, and enlightening (the gods). When pressed, whether near or at a distance, (Soma) enveloping protects us. The honeyed Soma is being strained out pure for Indra's drinking.

5. The every-where-going sister-consorts (the fingers), desirous of the mighty work (of bruising the plants), thrust (under the stones) the magnanimous lord, the mighty (moon-plant) Indu. O purified divinity, who shinest with ray after ray, when pressed for the gods, do thou bring among us all thy treasures. O purifier, pour down on us rain worthy of our praises, to enable us to serve the gods;[1] and let it come gathering around us, to provide for us food.

6. The preserver of men, the ever-watchful Agni, the possessor of wonderful might, was produced to cause prosperity anew to the worshippers; and the pure and shining god, lighted up by the priests with

---

[1] *Or* offer up our showers of adoring praises to the gods.

clarified butter, shines with an intense heaven-embracing flame. O Agni, Angiras Rishi found thee out when concealed as in a cave under the cover of every tree in the forest, and thou camest forth on being churned by his mighty strength. Hence, O emitter of heat, thou hast been called the Son of strength. The priests cause thee, Agni, the lighter up of the sacrifice, the first-born, who of old wast placed in thy sacred recess, and travellest with thy chariot in the same line with Indra and the gods, to shine forth in the mirthful assembly. Let then (Agni), the herald of the gods, and the prosperer of our religious acts, sit down on the sacred grass, to partake of the sacrifice.

7. O Mitra and Varuna, prosperers of sacrificial rites, these moon-plants have been pressed for you; therefore in this sacrifice hear my invocation. O possessors of radiance, without hate, immoveable, most excellent, who enter the hall of assembly, which has a thousand supporting pillars, (come hither). They two, the universal monarchs, whose food is melted butter and moon-plant juice, sons of Aditi, the givers of wealth, serve the guileless (performers of sacrifice).

8. Indra, who utters not a word against his worshippers, slew with the bones of the Rishi Dadhícha ninety times nine of his foes. Desirous of the Rishi's horse-head, which had its locality among

the mountains, he there discovered it in a lake.[1] When the time of the departure of the ever-moving Sun arrives, the light proceeds to take up its abode in the mansion of the moon.

9. This copious song of praise was produced by the hymning (Vaśishtha) for you, O Indra and Agni, and falls thick as the showers of rain from heaven. O Indra and Agni, do ye two hear the invocation of the chanter, and accept of his praises. O ye our rulers, give us the full reward of our religious services. O ye heroes, Indra and Agni, do not give us over to disgrace, nor to be the song of our enemies, nor to reproach.

10. O remover of sin, thou who art the supplier of strength, and the inebriator, strain out thy juice pure for the gods, for their drinking, and for the Maruts, and for Váyu. Soma shines brilliantly among the gods, seated on his own sacred Yoni,

---

[1] The Rishi here mentioned, according to the Bháshya, had been taught the Kavacha-vidyá (all-protective science), with a threatening, if he revealed it to any one, that he should have his head cut off. Wearied by the entreaties of the Aswiní Kumáras he revealed it to them, and suffered the threatened punishment. They, however, got a horse's head, and clapped it on his shoulders instead of his own. When the Rákshasas became rampant, Indra had to entreat this Rishi to lay down his life, that the bones of his new head might furnish weapons, the only ones by which his foes could be defeated. So dangerous is it even for a god to kill a sage!

as the rainer down of felicity, the revealer of enigmas, the beloved one, who undergoes the process of purification, and is incapable of sustaining injury. O subject of purification, thou who art laid hold of during the act of straining thee, and who proceedest with a resounding noise, enter into the sacred Yoni; through means of this ceremony enter the air-generating vessel.

11. O dripping Soma, day after day I long for thy friendship. O gray-coloured god, many Rákshasas run in upon me; do thou annihilate them all. To obtain thy friendship, O gray-coloured Soma, who distillest thy juice when pressed by day, and by night, do we bring here thy breasts (in bundles of thy twigs), and we approach thee shining with a radiance surpassing that of the Sun, as the eagle tribes (approach the luminary of day).

12. The purifier, the far-seeing Soma, who destroys all our murderous foes, the possessor of vast intelligence, our priests render glorious by their sacrificial rites. When he goes to his seat,[1] then Indra, the rainer of blessings, goes to drink the pressed juice, and afterwards departs for the immoveable abode (of the gods). O dripping Soma,

---

[1] The original is Yoni, "the womb where the spirit is generated;" but the Bhás. renders it generally 'seat.'

shower down to us great wealth, such as is coveted by thousands, and has been collected from every quarter of the world.

13. O Indra, drink the moon-plant juice; let that exhilarate thee, O possessor of the horses Harí, which the bruising-stone presses out by means of the arms of the juice-expressing priests, who lay tight hold on thee, as a man does on a horse. O Indra, possessor of the horses named Harí, let the intoxicating, sparkling liquor, which is thy due, and by which thou slayest our foes, pleasurably excite thee, the possessor of vast treasures. O possessor of riches, I, Vaśishṭha, celebrate thee in a song, which song of mine do thou favourably regard. Accept of these sacrificial viands offered thee in this sacrifice.

14. Our heroes in one united band are rendering brilliant, and bringing into view, to render us glorious, and bestow upon us imperishable riches, such as to confer on men renown when they have performed sacrifice, Indra, the subduer of hostile armies, the slayer of foes, the stern, the mighty, the ancient, the fleet. The Brahmans, as soon as they see the all-embracing Indra, who assumed the form of a ram, fall down before him, that they may celebrate his praise. Do ye, glorious chanters, who are devoid of malice, and ever eager for sacred song, shout together praises into the ear of Indra, in the

words of the sacred hymns. The singers unite to celebrate Indra, that he may come to the moon-plant banquet, when the lord of heaven, the sustainer of sacred rites, for the prosperity of his worshippers, comes in his might, and with his aids.

15. I praise that Indra who is the king of men, who journeys in a chariot which never varies from its course, who is the saviour of all our armies, the primeval divinity, and the slayer of Vritra. O Purohanmá, in whose substance a double quality resides,[1] for thy own preservation, render thy Indra glorious; since he is the holder of the thunderbolt, worthy of being reverently approached, mighty and radiant like the Sun.

16. The wise Soma, who is bruised between the two planks, and is famed for the performance of sacred rites, proceeds with a fleetness surpassing the most famous birds, along with the performers of the sacrifice. Soma enlightens (the heaven and the earth), the mighty son, the mighty mother, the pure offspring, the parent, the prosperer of the sacrifice. Thou, Soma, art excellent for the consumption of the man who lives in a place void of malice, and who sings thy praise; come therefore to our songs of praise.

---

[1] *i. e.* preservation for friends, and destruction for foes.

17. Thou, O divine purifier, art the most brilliant of beings; come, sounding, to confer immortality on the gods. It was thou by whom Dadhyang Rishi, when about to perform a nine months' sacrifice, enlarged his door for the gods, by whom the Brahmans obtain (their desire), by whom our hosts obtain food, with prosperity, bringing water for the satisfaction of the gods.

18. Soma, the purifier, flows down in many drops through the goat's-hair strainer, and, himself pure, keeps sounding in the presence of the singers. The priests by their hymns[1] purify the powerful Soma, who performs his frolics amid the sacred liquid, and sits above the sacred goat-hair mat; and the sages, in the three daily sacrifices, unitedly praise him on all sides. The desirer of food, the sprinkler, is being produced in the receiving-vessel, and like (a horse) springing (into battle), the purifier, uttering his voice, rushes forward.

19. Soma is flowing down pure; he is the creator of intellect, the creator of heaven, the creator of earth, the creator of fire, the creator of the Sun, the creator of Indra.[2] Soma, when he goes sounding to his holy place, is Brahmá among the gods, the fixer of their respective merits among the poets,

---

[1] Or adding *ti* to *dhi,* their fingers.

[2] Soma is here apparently identified with what the Hindus now term Brahm.

the Rishi among the Brahmans, the buffalo among horned animals, the hawk among the vulture tribe, the sword among cutting instruments. Soma the purifier, with vibratory motion, inspires us with songs and soul-moving hymns, sending forth as rivers a flood of sound. Soma, who sees the inward soul and is the rainer of felicity, sits down among us with his unmatched strength, and is well skilled in the matter of cows.[1]

20. Do ye come into the presence of your Agni, who grows great over the oblations, and is a most mighty and powerful protector. Let this Agni be present with us, as the carpenter is with the bodies he is about to reduce to form; and by his wisdom let us become famed. It is this Agni, who among the gods goes to the place where all estimable things are treasured up; let him come to us, bringing provisions.

21.[2] Drink, O Indra, this moon-plant juice; for it is most excellent and most exhilarating, and no death-bringing potion. In the sacrificial hall let the streams of the sparkling liquor distil into thee. There is no charioteer like thee, O Indra, who drivest thy pair of gold-green horses; there is no

---

[1] *i. e.* to increase our herds.

[2] Some copies have here, "In this place praise thou Agni, who is most celebrated by all chanters, and first honoured at sacrifices."

one like thee in might, nor are there any horses like thine. Do ye serve Indra with alacrity, sing the sacred hymns, and bow with reverence. Let the moon-plant juice be got ready for him, who holds the first place among the gods.

22. O Indra, possessor of the horses Harí, come hither, accept of our sacrifice, and bear it away. O thou resplendent and exhilarating god, drink of the expressed juice, pleasant as honey to the soul, and fitted to exhilarate the senses. Indra, fill thy belly anew with the expressed moon-plant juice, sweet as if distilled from the etherial regions; let the heavenly, exhilarating, pleasant-sounding liquor find a place with thee. Indra, like a friend, advanced to the front of the battle, and slew Vritra. He, like a hero, hewed down the hosts of the Dánavas, and, as a protector, subdued our foes, when he had enjoyed his moon-plant liquor.

[End of the fifth Adhyáya.]

SIXTH ADHYÁYA.

1. Pour out pure the cow-producing, wealth-producing, gold-producing, vegetable moon-plant juice, which is intermingled with the waters. Thou, O Soma, art a most heroic divinity; our priests have seated themselves to perform the worship of thee the omniscient. Thou, O Soma, art desired

by all men in every quarter; thou art the purifier, the rainer of the waters, to which thou proceedest in many drops. Let him strain out pure to us gold, with all kinds of wealth, and may we be ordained to live on earth. O imperial Soma, having yoked thy green swift-going (horses), thou makest thy way to all the inhabitants of the world. Let these thy horses distil the delicious shining liquid. O Soma, the officiating priests are standing engaged in the performance of thy rites.

2. O omniscient (Soma), the streams of thee the purifier, like the rays of the Sun, flow forth in abundance. O Soma, in whom the sweet juices reside, and who conferrest on us wisdom, thou distillest on all sides all valuable forms from the firmament, and sendest them to us. Manifested, O purifier, like the radiant Sun, thou proceedest to the receiving-vessel, uttering thy voice.

3. The purified radiant drops of moon-plant juice proceed in their course, and, mingled with the produce of the cow, mix with the holy waters. The moving juices proceed like torrents to the low grounds, and the purifying liquids encircle Indra, (and bring him to the sacrifice). O Soma, the purifier, the exhilarator[1] of Indra, thou art pro-

---

[1] *Or* intoxicator. The word usually refers to that incipient inebriation which excites the powers of mind and body.

ceeding forward on thy way, and, pressed by priests, art being brought as an offering (to the gods). Soma, when pressed by the stones, assumes his sacred form, and moves all around in the belly of Indra. O Soma, the exhilarator of men, who art laid hold of by men, flow down in purity, and pour forth songs of praise. O most powerful slayer of our foes, thyself pure, and the purifier of others, be the sweetener of the juice, the preserver of the gods, and the chastiser of sinners.

4. O all-wise Soma, who becomest pure in contact with the goat's-hair strainer, for the banquet of the gods, thou art the chastiser that subduest all our foes. He, the purifier, gives, without fail, food a thousand-fold more than they require, accompanied with herds of cows, to those that celebrate his praise. It is thou, O Soma, that purifiest and pourest forth our praises. Let that Soma give us food and all kinds of wealth with good-will. Pour out for the sacrificers fame-conferring, undecaying wealth, and bring food for the chanters. Thou, O purifying Soma, in the form of the wondrous Agni, glorious as a king, didst mingle thyself with our songs. Soma himself, though the principal divinity in the sacrifice, when among the waters is afflicted for the purpose of saving others,[1] and, after being

---

[1] The word for 'afflicted' is 'dushťara.' This is the first

pressed out pure by the hands of the priests, takes his seat in the receiving-vessel. O Soma, playing thy frolics like one begging a gift, thou arrivest at thy pure state, and bestowest prosperity-causing strength on him that celebrates thy praise.

5. Strain out for us over and over again, and in great abundance, thy juice in a nourishing stream, and bestow on us every valuable thing. O Soma, since to thee belongs the might, and to thee the provisions which are produced by thee in the form of the nourisher, do thou sit down on the love-producing sacred grass. O Soma, strain out for us in thy purifying stream, without fail, and by the speediest means, the wealth that consists in cows and horses. Do thou, the subduer of hundreds of foes, who conquerest but never art conquered, and who, as often as thou attackest, slayest thy enemies, flow forth pure (for us).

6. The sweet-juice-distilling streams are being prepared for our preservation; sit thou down with them on the sacred grass. When pressed, distil thyself for the drinking of Indra, proceeding by thy diversified paths, seating thyself in the womb of the sacrifice.[1] O Soma, most pleasant to the taste, and

---

passage in which the vicarious suffering of a deity is spoken of as beneficial to his worshippers.

[1] The vessel which receives the juice and in which the spirit is produced—the Yoni.

the conferrer of riches, do thou strain out for the descendants of Angiras the sparkling liquor.

7. Thy glories, O Agni, are manifested as the lightnings from a rainy cloud, or as the radiance of the morn when shed on the fields of corn or on the forests. Thou thyself puttest the food into our mouths. When, O Agni, stirred up by the wind, thou quickly fallest on the shining (wood), thou proceedest forward, surrounding the food provided for thee: and like as charioteers go separated from one another into the field of battle, so do the radiant emissions of thee, the undecaying divinity. O Agni, we and our assistant priests worship thee, and none other than thee, that we may receive a share in the oblations offered in this lower world, O thou mighty divinity, the giver of intelligence, the prosperer of the sacrifice, the beholder (of the gods), the subduer (of our foes), and the source of wisdom.

8. O Mitra and Varuna, your aid is unfailingly manifested in giving us abundance; and your favourable disposition towards us is most certainly worthy of our adoration. O Mitra and Varuna, void of enmity, we (sing praises) in your presence, to obtain food and a place of abode; may we through you obtain (prosperity). Preserve us, O Mitra and Varuna, with all kinds of preservation. O illustrious saviours, do ye save us, and grant

that by means of numerous sons we may subdue our foes.

9. O Indra, when standing by us in all thy mighty strength, thy whole face was agitated by its effects[1] when thou hadst drunk our moon-plant liquor. O Indra, when contending with our foes, the eyes of all in heaven and earth were tremblingly fixed on thee; but when thou becamest victorious over the enemy (their terror vanished). I esteem the voice which extends to the eight quarters of the earth, and even expands to the ninth (zenith regions), and which makes the sacrifice prosperous, still far below the praises of Indra.

10. O Indra and Agni, these songs celebrate you; do ye, the givers of happiness, drink the expressed juice. O heroes, there are in your possession a hundred thousand much-desired (horses) for the use of the institutor of the sacrifice. Come, O Indra and Agni, bringing them along with you. O heroes, Indra and Agni, come with them to this expressed moon-plant sacrifice, to drink the moon-plant juice.

11. Leaving thy native seat in the forest,[2] thou, O most glorious Soma, proceedest to the receiving-vessel, making a great and continued noise. Let

---

[1] This passage is intended to extol the strength of the spirit.

[2] *Or perhaps better*, sitting on thy native seat over the waters.

the drops of moon-plant juice, incorporating themselves with the waters, distil for Indra, for Váyu, for Varuna, for the Maruts, and for Vishnu. O Soma, whilst thou givest us food for our sons, cause to flow to us from every quarter wealth which shall be reckoned by thousands.[1]

12. Soma, when pressed, flows down through the elevated plain[2] of goats' hair, in a gold-coloured inebriating stream, with the speed of a mare. He who unites with the produce of the cow, flows down to mingle with that produce, and the moon-plant juice is combined with the milk. Like waters flowing into the sea, the sacred food proceeds to the receiving-vessel; and the inebriating Soma is pressed for the production of exhilaration.

13. O Soma, the purifier, do thou bring to us such celestial and terrestrial wealth as shall be worthy of admiration and worthy of praise. O rainer of blessings, who purgest from evil the life (of the pious), while with thy golden tinge thou resoundest over the sacrificial grass, sit down on thy native seat. Since you, Soma and Indra, are the possessors of all things, the protectors of the

---

[1] *i. e.* so abundant that the odd portions will not even be counted.

[2] Here *sánu* is used in a double sense (as above, *vana*, for 'water' or 'a forest'). There is a play upon the word, the goat's-hair strainer being compared to a mountain-top.

herds of cows, and lords paramount, do ye partake of the juice offered up in our sacred rites.

14. Indra, the slayer of Vritra, is extolled by our hymning heroes to obtain exhilaration and strength. Him then we invoke for aid in all our great struggles; and may he prevent us with his aids in every lesser conflict. Since, O Indra, thou art a hero, art of thyself an army, convey to us unobserved the vast (treasures of the enemy); and, since thou art the exalter of the depressed, bestow many gifts on the institutor of the sacrifice. When (our armies) go forth to battle, let them conquer, and bring back loads of riches, for the performer of thy sacrifices.

15. In like manner the (heavenly) cows, that shine together with Indra, drink of the sweet juice prepared in the sacrifice, and, accompanying the sender of rain, delight themselves together, and stay to enjoy the blessings of his government. Loving to be stroked by him, and of various colours, they mingle their milk with the moon-plant juice. These cows, beloved of Indra, hurl the destructive thunderbolt, and, fixed in their places, desire to live under the reign of Indra. Possessors of intellect, they maintain his strength by the nourishment (they yield), and make known his many mighty deeds, to lead (our foes) to reflect well ere (they attack us).

16. The mountain-inhabiting moon-plant, when pressed to produce the exhilarating beverage, attaining to its full growth in the waters, sits as a hawk on the receiving-vessel. The cows render pleasant by their milk the shining pressed beverage, purified by men, and desired by gods. And afterwards, as they adorn a horse whom they send into the battle, so let the priests render glorious this sweet juice, which they bring forth in the sacrifice for the prevention of death.

17. O lord of food, cause to shine among us the resplendent, mighty, nourishing, deity-desired liquor, and bring us in contact with the watery treasure, that floats in mid-air. O thou possessed of holy might, who art pressed by the planks, and like a king art the supporter of thy subjects, come to us and pour out pure to us from heaven an all-diffusive shower of rain; and be propitious to the rites (performed) by our host, who is eagerly desirous of cows.

18. (Soma) is the giver of life to the sacrifice, the son of the revered waters, that introduces into the sacrifice his resplendent person, and diffuses himself through the much-desired oblations, both here below and elsewhere. When Soma enters into Trita Rishi's secret room, he bows with reverence in the place where are the bruising planks, hard as stone; and afterwards (the priests) praise

him, their beloved (god), in the seven sacred metres. By means of his streams, he causes Indra, the giver of wealth, to come to the three daily sacrifices, performed by me Trita, and accompanied with pacificatory hymns; for our intelligent chanter knows to select the suitable hymns.

19. O Soma, when pressed, and endued with all thy surpassing sweetness, pour out in thy pure stream thy juice for Indra and Vishnu, and all the gods, that they may all join in our banquet. The guileless fingers (of the priests) press thy auburn person, O purifier, in the holy sacrifice, consisting of various rites, as the mother cow, while licking it, presses her newly-produced calf. O performer of mighty acts, thou sustainest heaven and earth. O purifier, when thou hast grown great, thou castest thy skin.[1]

20. The powerful, sparkling moon-plant liquor, the moving liquid flood, imparting strength to Indra, is now being purified for his delightful exhilaration. At the same time, the lord of strength slays the Rákshasas, and annihilates every foe, while he confers wealth (on the sacrificers). After being pressed by the stones, the moon-plant, (in the form of juice,) feeling its way obliquely through the hair-

---

[1] Probably an allusion to the serpent. Soma, or the spirit, leaves the moon-plant, and mingles as a liquor with the waters.

strainer, drips down pure in a sweet stream; and now an inebriating resplendent divinity obtains Indra's friendship, and flows forth for the exhilaration of the god. The resplendent god Soma, who renders holy our rites, is being purified, and by means of his juice comes in contact with the gods, while he overshadows the preservative rites, during the sacrifice, while the ten fingers, making him more forward, lead him from the mountain to where the goat's-hair strainer is placed.

21. O divine Agni, we light up thee, the shining indestructible divinity. In whatever part of the heavens thy flame, worthy of all praise, emits its radiance, from thence do thou bring food for those that celebrate thy praise. O Agni, lord of light, the sacrifice, accompanied with sacred hymns, is being offered up to thee, the radiant god. O possessor of all joy, destroyer (of foes), lord of men, bearer away of the oblation, it is being offered to thee; bring food to those who celebrate thy praise. O possessor of all joy, lord of men, thou receivest the oblation-presenting spoon and its cover both into thy mouth. O lord of strength, during the singing of the hymns, grant our desire, and bring food to those that celebrate thy praise.

22. (O singers), sing the great pacificatory psalter[1]

[1] In the original, Vrihat Sáma. This second division is the Vrihat Sáma.

in praise of the wise, mighty, food-providing, intelligent, praise-loving Indra. Thou, O Indra, art the subduer of foes, thou didst light up the Sun; thou art the creator of all things, the universal divinity, the mighty one. O Indra, thou wentest forth with thy radiance, illuminating the heavens, and lighting up the Sun. All the gods, through thy friendship, become subservient to our wishes.

23. The moon-plant is bruised for thee, O Indra. O possessor of might, overwhelmer of enemies, come fill us with animal vigour to the extent that the Sun fills the heavens with his rays. O slayer of Vritra, ascend thy chariot drawn by those gold-coloured horses that are yoked by pronouncing an incantation. Let the bruising-stone by its sound bring thy spirit graciously into our presence. Let his gold-coloured horses bring Indra, indomitable in might, to the eucharistic hymns and the sacrifice of Rishis and men.

[End of the sixth Adhyáya.]

SEVENTH ADHYÁYA.

1. The light of the sacrifice, the sweet, the beloved (liquor) is being distilled in purity. It is the preserver of the gods, the creator (of happiness), and the source of great wealth. It is that joy-inspiring, most inebriating, sense-delighting liquor, which

brings to us the treasures of heaven and earth, and of the middle regions. The possessor of all things, the lord of heaven, the all-seeing, who moves in a hundred streams, flows down with a resounding noise into the receiving-vessel; and the gold-coloured divinity sits in the house of his friend, being rendered pure by the conducting hairs of the strainer, and becomes to him the rainer of blessings. O Soma, when purified, thou drippest down, and movest into the presence of waters, and art joined with fluency of speech; and, when honoured as the principal person, thou movest in front of the rays of light.[1] In thy full suit of armour thou honourest the field of battle, and marchest back in front of the stores of (our enemies') supplies, as often as thou art pressed by the performers of the moon-plant sacrifice.

2. The fleet, shining, every-where-diffused drops of moon-plant juice, begging for cows, horses, and heroes, are being prepared. Rendered shining by the priests, and purified by their arms, they drop down pure through the goat-hair sieve. Let them, O Soma, pour out pure for thy sacrificing host all heavenly, earthly, and air-born treasures.

3. Quickly strain out pure, O Soma, the holy

[1] The meaning is, water, &c., are obtained by these rites, in which Soma is honoured.

juice desired by the gods; and, O shining juice, enter into Indra. O rainer of felicity, most illustrious Soma, cause to come to us the mighty waters, and sit down on thy sacred seat,[1] for thou art our supporter. Soma, the performer of glorious actions, milks out the delightful sweet juice, the stream of the pressed producer of wealth, and then overshadows the sacred waters. When thou, (O Soma,) art enveloped with the produce of the cow, the mighty dripping waters flow into thee, the mighty one. The collector of liquids, the sustainer of all things, the supporter of heaven, Soma, desirous of union with us, combined with water, is being purified in the holy place. The rainer of felicity, the gold-coloured, the mighty one, who resembles a friend, and is worthy of being worshipped, shines with a lustre like that of the Sun. The rite-loving songs are rendered holy by thy might, O Soma, and with them thou art adorned for thy work of exhilaration. We implore the presence of the lord of the world to produce in us the excitement destructive to our foes, and we desire thy presence for thy own exaltation. Thou art the giver of cows, O Soma, the giver of horses, the giver of heroes, and the giver of food; the soul of the sacrifice, who continuest the same from the days of old.

---

[1] The original is Yoni.

Pour out for us, Soma, in a sweet stream, like showers of rain, the sense-stimulating juice.

4. O purifying Soma, mighty provider of food, bestow gifts (on the gods), and conquer (the Rákshasas), and afterwards grant us prosperity. Grant us strength and wisdom and merit, and slay the murderous crew: afterwards, grant us prosperity. The purifying priests are straining out pure the moon-plant juice to Indra for his drinking: afterwards, &c. Do thou, by thy wisely-ordered plans and protection, cause us to reach the world of the Sun: afterwards, &c. Through thy wisely-ordered plans and protection, may we see the Sun through all ages: afterwards, &c. O Soma, possessor of splendid armour, rain down upon us the abundant wealth of the two worlds: afterwards, &c. O Soma, who art incapable of injury in the field of battle, and art the subduer of foes, rain down on us wealth: afterwards, &c. O purifier, in this manifold reward-conferring ceremony, they have magnified thee by the sacrificial rites: therefore, do thou grant us prosperity. O Soma, bring wealth worthy of being extolled, and that moves all things, accompanied with horses; and, at the same time, grant us prosperity.

5. The preserver, the exhilarator, flows down in a stream of pressed nourishing (liquid). The preserver, the exhilarator, flows down. The goddess,

who bestows wealth, knows to save the man (who offers sacrifice). The preserver, &c. We take possession of the thousands (of hoards of treasure), which belong to Drusrya and Purushanta. The preserver, &c.

6. These moon-plants, the subject of our hymns of praise, flow down in a stream of most exhilarating liquor, to procure for us strength. O purifier, thou distillest streams of enriching milk for the banquet of the gods; flow down to us pure as a nourishing (liquid). Distil to us the all-satisfying, every-where-praised, nourishing produce of the cow, as often as thou art celebrated by me Jamadagni.

7. We direct this hymn of praise to the honoured producer of wealth, with all the nice discrimination (the carpenter employs in polishing) a chariot; for our properly-directed chanter is always in a happy mood in the sacred assembly. O Agni, grant through thy friendship that we may never be slain. We bring forward the wood for fuel,[1] and offer up the oblation when we remember thee, fortnight after fortnight. Prosper our rites abundantly, to procure for us long life. O Agni, grant, &c. We are enabled to light up thee, and carry on our sacred rites to completion; for by thee the gods eat up the offered oblations: do thou therefore bring to us the

---

[1] Twenty-one pieces of the palás-wood.

sons of Aditi. And, O Agni, grant that through thy friendship we may never be slain.

8. I praise you unitedly and severally, Mitra, and Varuna, and Aryamá, the destroyers of our foes, every day at the rising of the Sun. Let this hymn of praise be productive of protection from foes, and strength accompanied with treasures of gold, as well, ye wise ones, as for obtaining a share in the sacrifice. May we, who are thine, O resplendent Mitra, and thine, O Varuna, live happily, and obtain bread and water, as well as our hymning priests.

9. Cleave asunder all who hate us, slay in war all who oppose us, and bring to us health worthy of our desires. Every one knows the amount, and the particulars in the order of succession, of the wealth which thou hast bestowed on many. Therefore, bring us, &c. O Indra, bring the wealth, worthy of being desired, which is stored up in a strong immoveable treasury, which cannot be broken up.

10. O Indra and Agni, since you at every season are the preparers of my sacrifice, and, when purified, engage in the sacrificial conflict, regard my oblations. O Indra and Agni, destroyers of your foes, who travel in chariots, the slayers of enemies, the invincible, regard my oblations. O Indra and Agni, the offerers of the sacrifice have prepared

this exhilarating sweet juice for you; therefore regard my oblations.

11. O Soma, thou art most pleasant to the taste; therefore, having taken thy seat on the reverential spirit-producing seat, distil it out pure for Indra and the Maruts. The learned men acquainted with the laws of elocution magnify thee, the sustainer (of all things), and our common priests unite in purifying thee. O thou, who presidest over sacred rites, let Mitra, Aryamá, and the Maruts drink of the juice thou yieldest when distilled.

12. O beautiful-handed Soma, when purified, thou makest thy way into the receiving-vessel. O purified Soma, it is thou that distillest the yellow, abundant, much-desired treasure. O purified (Soma), who art rendered pure by percolation through the goat's-hair strainer, thou makest a noise like a bull when pouring down into the waters. O purified Soma, thou goest shining with the produce of the cow to the well-constructed mansions of the gods.

13. The ten fingers purify this Soma, whose mother is the waters, and he marches along with the gods. The pressed moon-plant juice accompanies Indra, Váyu, and the solar rays, into the holy place. O sweet-flavoured, fortune-bringing Soma, distil thyself in our sacrifice for Bhaga, for Váyu, for Púshá, for Mitra, and for Varuna.

14. Let us have rich cows, the producers of

abundance of food, and let Indra delight himself with us, that we, the possessors of food, may rejoice on their account. When, O upholder (of all things), we can indeed lay hold of one like thee, to whom we can present our petitions, thou throwest in the objects of our desire, with the constancy that the spokes of a wheel tend to the axle. O performer of many merit-conferring acts, thou castest in the wealth desired by the singers, with the constancy that all the movements (of the cart) tend to the axle.

15. We, day by day, call on thee, the performer of praiseworthy acts, with the regularity that people call on the milch-cow to the milking. O drinker of the moon-plant juice, come to our three daily sacrifices, and drink the Soma juice. Let the delight of thee, possessed of all riches, equal his who presents cows to Brahmans. Do not leave us, to show thyself elsewhere.

16. O Indra, like the luminous morn, thou fillest both worlds with thy radiance. Thee, who art the superior of the superior powers, and the lord of men, did the divine mother produce; thee did the propitious mother bring forth. Thou, O all-wise, hast the strength of the iron rod that guides the elephant. O possessor of riches, as a goat lays hold on the twigs with his fore-foot, so dost thou press down thy enemies: for thee did the divine

mother, &c. Bring down the might of the man who would slay us, or give us pain, and place him who would enslave us under our feet: for thee did the divine mother, &c.

17. The resounding, gold-coloured moon-plant juice is dripping down on every side in the holy place. Thou, (O Soma,) art the distributor of all things amid the exhilarated priests. Thou art most affectionate to us, and most intelligent, and givest us the sweet liquor produced from the grain. Thou art, &c. All the gods who love one another have obtained in thee a plenteous draught. Thou art, &c.

18. It is Soma who brings to the offerer of sacrifice treasures of riches and food, and gives him a suitable place of abode. We prepare the moon-plant juice, of which Indra, the Maruts, Aryamá, and Bhaga drink, and with which we bring into our presence Mitra and Varuna and Indra, to afford us mighty aids.

19. O my friends, celebrate the purifier, who is manifested for the exhilaration of the gods, pleasing him with offerings and hymns, as (the nurse does) a child. As calves (shine when licked) by their mothers, so are the moon-plants made to shine (by being sprinkled) with water; and the preserver of the gods, the exhilarator, is rendered glorious by our hymns. This most exhilarating pressed moon-

plant juice is prepared for nourishment, for strength, for the sacrificial banquet, and for the gods.

20. The shining expressed drops of moon-plant juice, most quick in their descent, friendly, guileless, and skilled in sacred narration,[1] and which tend to heaven, are being distilled in purity for our benefit. These drops are those of the pressed, wisdom-conferring, cream-united moon-plant juice, which move among the sacred waters, imperishable, and, like the Sun, worthy of our adoration. Moving in a tortuous path, well pressed by the stones, and known by his position over the bull's hide, Soma, the procurer of wealth, utters his voice so as to be heard on all sides while bringing us provisions.

21. O Soma, strain out pure for us, in this thy holy stream, the various kinds of wealth in the presence of those who celebrate thy praise, and run down into the liquid-containing vessel; for to this, (Aditya,) the origin of all things, and (Indra), the performer of numerous sacrifices, bend their steps. May Soma give us heroes. Strain out pure for us in a clear stream thy own essence, worthy of all praise, in the holy place, where thy sound is heard, and let the destroyer of our foes strike down to us sixes of thousands of treasure, for victory in the

[1] Alluding, I suppose, to the noise they make in falling down into the vessel below.

field of battle, as men shake down showers of ripe fruit from a tree. Let his (arrow)-raining, (foe)-prostrating, mighty, joy-bringing, destroying acts be manifested both among those who fight on horseback and those who engage in close fight, and by them let him cause the enemy to sleep the sleep of death; and let him beat off our foes, and drive back those who neglect sacred rites.

22. O Agni, be thou near to encircle us all around, as our saviour, and as the conferrer on us of happiness. O all-resplendent Agni, who assignest us a place of abode, who livest diffused in food, display thyself in our presence, and give us food.

23. May we obtain all material substances, and may Indra and all the gods be at our nod. May Indra, along with the Adityas, bestow upon us the materials for sacrifice, and strength of body, and offspring. Let Indra, along with the Adityas and Maruts, and attended with his company, furnish us with medicinal substances.

24. Do ye with zeal in our presence perform the service of Indra.

[End of the seventh Adhyáya.]

EIGHTH ADHYÁYA.

1. As the Rishi Uśana speaks his poetical compositions, so let our divine priest accurately narrate the birth of the gods. The performer of mighty acts, the possessor of pure radiance, comes forward like a boar, raising his voice, and scattering the earth with his feet. The highly devout company of sages quickly repair, at the sound of the noise of bruising the plants, to the house where the sacrifice is being offered; and my friends celebrate with proper intonations the god worthy of our host, the invincible, pure Soma. Soma, putting forth his far-famed speed, travels, though merely as if in sport, and without any effort, so that no roadster can come up to him. The possessor of penetrating radiance diffuses splendour in abundance, appearing by day of a gold-colour, and by night luminous.

2. During the time of bruising, the drops of moon-plant juice, sounding like a chariot, or like a horse desiring food, proceed forward for the purpose of bestowing wealth (on the sacrificers).—When marching with the speed of a chariot (to the oblation-hall), the arms of the priests sustain him, (Soma,) as those of labourers their loads. As kings are glorified by hymns of praise, and a sacrifice by the seven priests, so is Soma by the

produce of the cow. The sweet moon-plants, when pressed, flow in a stream, and with a loud voice, for the production of inebriation. The juices flow down during the time of bruising with a noise for the glorious toper Indra, who gives its splendour to the morning. The chanters of the sacred hymns, the men who bear the juice of the rainer of felicity, now shut the ancient doors. As the seven oblation-offering priests surround the place of the one Soma, so do his consorts strive to please him. In order that I may behold the Sun with my eyes, I place Soma, the navel of the sacrifice, in my navel, and milk out the juice of the prosperer of all our works. Indra beholds, (O Soma,) with his eye the beloved manifestation of thy glorious person, when placed in the cavity of the human body.

3. Quantities of moon-plant juice, bringing prosperity, and knowing what is adapted to this sacrifice, are being prepared, and enter by the way of the solemn rite into the service of the gods. The soul of the sacrifice, the sweet-savoury mighty Soma, is worshipped by oblations, and goes to bathe in the sacred waters. He who raises his voice is worthy of being offered to the gods; the sovereign, the rainer of felicity, the faithful, the indestructible, when he goes to his place of abode, utters a sound upon the sacred waters. When he who knows how to perform all rites, who pours out pure for us our might,

proceeds to where the sacred song is heard, the provider of food is there present, desiring our food. The pure Soma advances against our foes, as a king against his rebellious subjects, when the performers of the sacred rites send him forward. The gold-coloured, the beloved Soma, mixed with the waters, sits all around on the goats' hair, and himself uttering a sound, is worshipped by song. He who is filled with joy through the performance of this sacred rite, goes exhilarated to wait on Váyu, Indra, and the twin sons of Aświni. Streams of sweet juice flow into Mitra, Varuna, and Bhaga. Those then who are acquainted with Soma approach them with pleasure. O heaven and earth, for the obtaining of the sweet, nourishing juice, do ye put into our possession wealth, provisions, and flocks of cattle.

4. (O Soma), we render homage to thy pleasure-producing, wealth-collecting, saving, much-desired might. We worship thee, the exhilarator, the eminent, the wise, the celebrated, the preserver, the much-desired. O possessor of great riches, the great, the wise, we ask for our sons wealth and intelligence, while we worship thee the preserver, the much-desired.

5. The (priestly) gods are producing Agni, the head of the heavens, who ascends from earth, who dwells in heaven, who is born on account of the

sacrifice, who is full of legendary lore, the brilliant god, who is the guest of men, and the mouth of the gods, and our saviour. When thou, (O Agni.) art produced, all the gods move towards thee,[1] as a father to his son; and, O (Vaiśwánara), friend of all men, when thou shinest forth as the preserver of all, (the Brahmans) obtain immortality through these thy rites. Our gods greatly praise thee, the navel of the sacrifices, the abode of wealth, the mighty receiver of oblations, and produce thee, who dwellest in all men, who art the chariot of the oblations, the originator of the sacrifice.

6. O ye priests, celebrate Mitra and Varuna in songs at the height of your voice, and do ye both, possessed of great strength, come to the long-continuing sacrifice. Ye who are the universal lords, the womb of the waters, yourselves divinities, and mighty among the gods, you can impart to us the immense wealth of heaven and earth: we adore that great power of yours, which is great even among divinities.

7. Come, O Indra, famed for thy varied radiance; these goblets of moon-plant juice await thy coming, which have to-day been rendered holy by the fingers (of the officiating priests). Indra, come, and listen to the sacred hymns of the offerers of expressed

---

[1] *Or* all the (priestly) gods unite in praising thee.

moon-plant juice, moved by our solemn rites and the worship of the attendant Brahmans. Indra, possessor of the gold-coloured horses, come quickly to hear our sacred hymns; accept of our moon-plant juice and sacrificial viands.

8. Praise that Agni, who, when by his radiant flame he encircles all the forests, renders them black by the touch of his tongue. He who throws into the shining divinity propitious offerings for Indra, will receive from him pleasant, preserving rains for the production of glorious crops of corn. Indra and Agni, do ye two furnish for us strengthening food and swift horses, that we may supply you with oblations.

9. O Soma, thou goest forward into the beautifully formed belly of Indra, and, as a friend, fillest without overflowing the sounding cavity. As a male among females, so does Soma by a hundred winding paths make his way into the receiving-vessel.[1] The meditative, joy-loving, praise-loving singers are moving about in the thatched oblation-hall, and the chanters are celebrating the gold-coloured juice, which the cows by their milk make more suitable for use. O brilliant Soma, cause the collected abundant store of provisions and liquid nourishment to flow to us in thy stream; which

[1] *i. e.* winding through the hairs of the strainer.

liquid nourishment, in the three daily sacrifices, milks out for us a well-provisioned, powerful, excited race of renowned heroes.

10. He alone who performs sacrifice makes Indra his friend, who ever prospers his worshipper, is extolled by all, is the invincible, the subduer of foes by his great might, and is able in the engagement to overpower his opponent. I praise Indra, who is the subduer of foes, and fierce and irresistible in the war, where he displays his majesty, and where the delighters in sacrifice reverently adore him, and heaven and earth bow before him.

11. O my friends, sit ye down, and sing hymns to the purifier; adore him with offerings, that ye may adorn him, as a father does his son (with jewels). Do ye bring to perfection in the maternal waters this juice, the produce of your house, the preserver of the gods, the causer of exhilaration, the producer of strength to both worlds, as the cow (brings forth) her calf. Do ye purify the strengthening juice, to procure rapidity of motion and nourishment (to the gods); and, since it is most beneficial, prepare it for Mitra and Varuna.

12. The strengthening Soma flows obliquely through the holy goat's-hair strainer. The strengthening juice, of most powerful energy, mingled with the waters, and fitted for use with the produce of the cow, flows down. O Soma, bruised by the

stones, and strained by the priests, descend into the belly of Indra.

13. Those portions of moon-plant juice which are prepared at a distance, and those that are prepared near at hand, and those which abound in the lake Śaryanavat, are all for thee, O Indra, and those which are prepared in the country of Árjíka and Kritwa, and on the banks of the rivers (Saraswatí, &c.), and by the five tribes of men. May those pressed, brilliant floods of moon-plant juice cause rain and an army of heroes to flow down pure to us from heaven.

14. O Agni, I Vatsa wish to bring down thy spirit from the lofty, shining heavens. I wish to bring thee hither by a soul-delighting song. Thy eye is steadily fixed on many regions, and thou art the lord of all those regions: therefore we call on thee in all our conflicts. Desirous of food, we in all our conflicts call to our aid Agni, who possesses treasures accumulated in his wars.

15. O Indra, performer of many meritorious deeds, beholder of all things, bring to us might and wealth. We invoke the hero who sends down rain. Thou, (O Indra,) art to us a father, thou art to us a mother. O assigner to us of our place of abode, and performer of many meritorious deeds, we desire the felicity that resides in thee. O powerful Indra, invoked by many worshippers, the

conferrer of strength, we call upon thee when engaged in war; do thou grant us heroic armies.

16. O Indra, glorious attendant on sacrifices, the wealth thou canst give I have nowhere in this world. O possessor of riches, bring treasures in both thy hands. O Indra, bring that food thou esteemest well worthy of praise, that we may become the recipients of thy bounty. By that much-extolled, famed, mighty, unflinching spirit, which thou possessest, O attendant on sacrifices, present us with provisions for our acceptance.

[End of the eighth Adhyáya.]

NINTH ADHYÁYA.

1. The Maruts in bands purify and adorn the intelligent, newly-produced infant Agni. And the bard, for by the regularity of his sound Soma proves himself to be a bard, comes sounding to the holy vessel. The possessor of an all-observant mind, who manifests himself to men, the accepter of all, who is worshipped by thousands, the rectifier of the mistakes of poets, the venerable, much-praised Soma, who desires to dwell in the third world (the heavenly), encircles with glory the glorious Indra. The much-praised hawk, and powerful falcon, Soma, moving between the ex-

pressing planks, seated in the sacrificial ladle, and performing many frolics, the consumer (of the produce) of the cow, moving quickly, lays hold of his weapons; and, when worshipped, the adorable god honours with his presence the sky that sends down the waters, as well as the fourth (the lunar) region.

2. These moon-plants distil the juice that Indra dearly loves, and increase his vigour. The purifying ladle-contained drops of juice move towards Váyu and the sons of Aświni. May they impart to us abundant vigour (for a heroic army). O pure Soma, send, in order to procure for us wealth, the spirit of Indra, for I have set myself down on the sacred seat of the gods. The ten fingers strain thee out pure, the seven priests send thee forward, and the learned chanters inspire thee with delight. We consecrate thee for the exhilaration of the gods, along with the produce of the cow, when we have well prepared thy newly-produced felicity. The brilliant gold-coloured divinity completely veils himself with garments formed from the produce of the cow. O Soma, pour out to us the wealth of the rich, slay all that hate us, and procure for us the friendship of Indra. We obtain food and offspring while waiting on thee, the observer of men, the beholder of all things, who art quaffed by Indra. O Soma, pour rain from heaven, cover

the earth with corn, and supply us with strength in the battle.

3. Soma, the purifier, with his thousand streams passing through the goats' hair, drops down into the well-cleaned vessel of Váyu and Indra. O ye who desire preservation, do ye celebrate the purifying, wisdom-bestowing moon-plant liquor, well prepared for the banquet of the gods. The (goblets of) moon-plant liquor, possessed of surpassing power, and celebrated in our sacred hymns, are being consecrated for the banquet of the gods to obtain for us food. O Soma, that we may obtain provisions,[1] do thou distil out for us supplies of food, and such surpassing bodily vigour as shall make (our faces) shine. As fleet horses urged on by their riders to the war, so are the swift-flowing streams of moon-plant juice, which are prepared by the priests over the goat's-hair strainer, that we may obtain food. Let these pressed, shining moon-plants distil to us thousands of treasure, and surpassing bodily vigour. The sounding drops of moon-plant juice flow down with the speed that lowing cows run to their calves, and are again borne up by the arms of the priests. For the abundant satisfaction of Indra, the purifying juice prepared for him utters its voice. Do thou, O

---

[1] *Or* victory in our wars.

Soma, slay all our foes. Do ye, pure, all-seeing slayers of those who refuse to offer sacrifice, sit down on the sacrificial seat.[1]

4. To form part of the sacrifice, these delight-inspiring (goblets of) expressed moon-plant juice are being prepared for Indra. Our wise men call in hymns upon Indra to come to the drinking of the Soma, as cows do upon their calves. The spirit-distilling Soma sits on his seat on the wave of the sacred sea, and, as the god of wisdom, he resides in speech. Soma, the all-seeing, the all-wise, the prosperer of all our works, is worshipped by us in the navel of heaven, amid the goats' hair.[2] When the moon-plant juice is put within the sacred receiving-vessel, the god Soma enters into it. When the god Soma enters the sweet-juice-containing vessel, he utters a sound that, passing through mid-air, strikes the heavens above. When daily praised, the lord of forests, who sends auxiliaries to men, (drinks in) the milk of praise which our sages yield. O purifying Soma, pour down on us in a stream thousand-folds of brilliant, happiness-conferring wealth. O performer of glorious acts, intelligent, pressed Soma, from thy distant

---

1 Addressed to Soma, or to the other gods.

2 Referring to the strainer, which is elevated at some distance above the ground.

place in the heavens do thou regard us, and send us down in a stream all delightful things.

5. As the noise of the waves of the sea, or the sound of an arrow in its flight, so do thou send forth thy quickly-moving voice. The voices of the chanters of the three Vedas, desirous of engaging in the sacrifice, rise aloft as often as thou, desirous of mortal birth, ascendest the elevated goat's-hair strainer. The priests, straining by means of the goat's-hair sieve, send down on every side the beloved, green, stone-expressed, purifying, sweet, dripping liquid. O most exhilarating god, preserver of religious rites, pour down into the sacred vessel thy juice in a stream that may enter the belly of Indra, the object of our adoration. O most inebriating god, distil thyself pure, and, beautified with the shining produce of the cow, enter the belly of Indra.

6. Distil, in this rite, juice for the banquet of Indra, which (through its exhilarating power) slew in battle (by the hands of Indra) ninety times nine of his foes. In one day Soma slew Sambara, and destroyed his cities for Divodása, the supporter of religious rites, and then subjected to his will Divaśa, Turvaśa, and Yada. O Soma, possessor of horses, send us cavalry, and wealth consisting in abundance of cows, and gold; and pour out for us manifold stores of food.

7. Soma, having slain our murderous foes and those who do not give gifts, proceeding to the well-cleansed vessel of Indra, flows forth pure. O purifying Soma, bring us great wealth, slay our murderous foes, bestow upon us the fame that accompanies heroic descendants. O Soma, hundreds of foes cannot slay thee, when desirous of bestowing wealth, and purified, thou comest to give gifts.

8. O Soma, descend with that stream with which thou lightedst up the Sun; do thou descend, and send water for the use of man. It is Soma that yokes the horses of the Sun, when he is about to move through the heavens over the abode of men. "Soma is my master," says the Sun, and yokes his gold-coloured horses to the chariot, for the purpose of departing.

9. (O ye gods), cause your brilliant Agni, who is served by all the other fires, and is worthy of oblations, to assume his form of messenger in this faultless sacrifice: for he takes up his abode among men, is the receiver of oblations; whose brilliance is scorching, who is fed with clarified butter, and is our purifier. Uttering a noise like a horse when satisfied with grass, the mighty divinity, breaking over his bonds, fixes himself in some suitable place; and then, O Agni, thy brilliance, following the course of the wind, moves along, and the road thou followest is darkened. O

Agni, the immortal, shining radiance of thy newborn, rain-sending flames rise aloft; and thou, O Agni, in the form of flame and smoke, as the messenger of the gods, ascendest to heaven, and enterest the presence of the divinities.

10. We render that Indra powerful for the slaying of our foe, Vritra. Let him who is the rainer of felicity now rain down on us wealth. Indra was created to confer gifts. He is the most mighty, appointed to reside in the mighty Soma. He is a most illustrious god, the recipient of praise, and worthy to drink the moon-plant juice. He is sharpened like a Vajra by praise, and powerful and unconquered, the fierce hero, returning unwounded, and is desirous of bestowing gifts.

11. O ye priests, bring the moon-plant juice pressed out by the stones into the holy vessel, and purify it for Indra's drinking. O Soma, these gods and the Maruts are consuming thy sweet, purifying nourishment. O Soma, press out the most excellent, the most pleasant moon-plant juice, equal to Amrita, for Indra, the holder of the thunderbolt.

12. The sustainer of the heavens flows down, who requires to be produced anew while he assumes the form of juice. The infuser of strength into gods, and receiver of delight from man, the gold-coloured god, when produced, exhausts his

strength in frolics among the sacred waters, like a horse with his rider. As a warrior takes up in his hands his weapons, so Soma, desirous of sweet oblations, mounting his chariot, drives off for the cow-walks (to collect cows for the milk required in the sacrifice). And he who infuses strength into Indra is put into the holy food by our sacred rites, and is adorned by the hymns of our learned priests. O pure Soma, assuming all thy greatness, enter the belly of Indra in a full wave; and as lightning descends from the clouds, so flow thou down upon the two worlds, and measure out, on account of our works, abundance of provisions.

13. Although, O Indra, thou art invoked by men in the east, west, north, and south, yet, O mighty god, thou art present in the sacrifice of king Anu; and influenced by the merits of our many priests, thou, O subduer of foes, art present also with king Turvaśa. Or, shouldest thou be enjoying thyself at the banquet of king Ruma,[1] or Raśama, or Śyávaka, or Kripa, yet when the sons of Kanu, who bear the sacred viands, urge thee hither, do thou come, O Indra.

---

[1] These names seem descriptive of the nations bordering on the country of the Hindus; perhaps the nations on the Indus to the west, the Tartars to the north, the Tamulians to the south, and the Burmese or Chinese to the east.

14. Let Indra hear both our Rig and Sáma Veda hymns, which are sung in his presence; and let the mighty one for our society, and actuated by his own greatness of soul, come to the drinking of the moon-plant juice. Thee, shining with thy own radiance, and sending down on the two worlds thy rain, their inhabitants ever as suppliants approach, while thou sittest down as chief among the gods, with all thy mind intent on drinking the moon-plant beverage.

15. O divine (Soma), pour down thy juice, and let thy exhilarating might enter the long-lived Indra, and at the same time ascend into Váyu with thy upholding juice. O purifying Soma,[1] thou seizest the much-praised wealth (of our foes), and, when thou hast slain our foes, thou flowest down pure.

16. [*First line translated before.*] O bestower of a place of abode, we wish a portion of thy much-desired, abode-conferring wealth. O steady mover, grant that we, who delight in thee, may always be very near thy stores of food. Soma, who distils exhilarating juice through the goats' hair, when pressed, flows down on all sides; and he who delights in the produce of the cow, raised on high,

---

[1] It is easily seen that Soma is the moon-plant or its juice personified. He is also identified with the moon.

moves in a stream during the sacrifice, like a flood of light.

17. O Soma, mighty god, the sea (where the spirit collects), the father of all, distil thyself out pure for the nourishment of all the bodies of the gods. O Soma, thou shining divinity, flow out pure for the gods, and for heaven and earth, and the happiness of man. Thou art the supporter of heaven, worthy of being used as a beverage, and a powerful divinity; therefore pour thyself out pure in this rightly-performed sacrifice.

18. O Agni, I praise you, my beloved guest, dear as a friend, and valuable as a chariot. Ye (terrestrial) gods, who have with solemn rites placed Agni in his two receptacles[1] among men, do ye extol him, and be by him extolled, as two poets do to one another. (O god), who art ever-young, do thou preserve the heroes that belong to the performer of this sacrifice, do thou hear our songs, and along with our own persons preserve our sons.

19. O beloved Indra, conqueror of foes, incapable of being concealed, great as a mountain, superior to every other being, and lord of heaven; O faithful drinker of the moon-plant juice, thou art supreme over heaven and earth, thou art the

---

[1] The Áhavaníya and Gárhapati receptacles, or heaven and earth.

exalter of the institutor of the moon-plant sacrifice, and the lord of heaven. Thou art in truth the destroyer of all the enemies' cities, the slayer of the Rákshasas, the prosperer of men, and the lord of heaven.

20. Thou hast ever been the cleaver of cities, art ever-young, art all-intelligent, and of unmeasured strength. Indra, thou art the upholder of all sacred rites, the bearer of the thunderbolt, and extolled by us in manifold ways. Thou, O Indra, didst enter the cave of the cow-(stealing) Bala; the injured, terrified gods found a refuge in thee. Sing in hymns of praise with all your might to Indra the supreme, whose gifts are lavished in thousands, and even in greater abundance.

[End of the ninth Adhyáya.]

TENTH ADHYÁYA.

1. The collector of the waters spreads himself all around: the guardian deity that at first sustained the waters aloft, and created the tribes of men, is now the rainer down of felicity: this mighty, expressed, all-supporting Soma is in the holy place on the table-land of the goat's-hair strainer, rising to his magnificence. O purifying, divine Soma, cheer Mitra and Varuna, that they may confer on

us food and wealth. Cheer, O divine Soma, their mightinesses the Maruts. Cheer all the gods; cheer heaven and earth. The adorable Soma, when he honours the gods with his presence, becoming the womb of the waters, performs a mighty work. It is this purifying god that infused might into Indra, and this brilliant divinity begot in the Sun his luminous rays. This immortal god, like a bird, flies to his seat in the juice-receiving vessel. This resplendent god, when praised by the learned Brahmans, dips himself in the waters, and bestows valuable gifts on the institutor of the sacrifice. This pure, heroic Soma, like some warrior going forth, is desirous to obtain for us, in union with strength, all valuable things. This pure, dripping divinity desires a chariot (to come to the sacrifice), desires to bestow (on us gifts), and raises his voice aloud.

2. This pure, dripping divinity, like a bay horse, is adorned for the battle by our hymning, sacrifice-desiring priests. This divinity, sustaining no injury from the fingers (of the priests), overtakes all our foes. He who is the purifier, uttering a sound, speeds his way in a full stream to heaven, leaving the earth behind. The purifier, the prosperer of sacrifices, who never can be slain, passes on to heaven, leaving the earth behind. He who is the gold-coloured, shining divinity, and was born in

ancient times, has been pressed for the gods, and is distilling in the holy place. He who is the performer of many rites, who has submitted to mortal birth, who produces the sacrificial viands, is now being pressed, and is flowing down in a pure stream.

3. He, the heroic Soma, when pressed by the priests' fingers in the solemn rite, proceeds in his swift chariot to the seat of Indra.[1] He causes many rites to be performed for the splendid banquet of the gods, where the immortals crowd around. Him mortals strain out into the receiving-vessel, though originally pure; and there he affords for them abundant nourishing draughts. He is first consecrated, then carried through the assembly by a holy path, then the priest that bears him pours him out as an oblation. He, the powerful god, the lord of fluids, advances with golden, shining rays. He shakes his sharp horns as some bull chief of the herd, and collects riches for us by his might. He, arriving at the proper juncture, wholly discomfits the encircling (Rákshasas), and comes down upon their murderous bands. The ten fingers send forth this gold-coloured divinity, arrayed in becoming armour, and the causer of great exhilaration, to prosecute his journey.

---

[1] Either in heaven, or in the sacrificial vessel.

4. He who is the rainer of felicity and the fleet divinity proceeds through the goat's-hair strainer for the purpose of producing manifold stores of food. The fingers of Trita Rishi press forwards by means of the bruising-stones the gold-coloured moon-plant juice for Indra's drinking. Coming with the quickness of a hawk, he takes up his abode among the tribes of men, and proceeds with the eagerness of a paramour to his mistress. This exhilarating (spirit) is the son of heaven, and is the Soma juice that enters the hair-strainer. The gold-coloured god, the sustainer (of all things), expressed for the drinking (of the gods), flows down with a noise to his beloved seat (in the receiving-vessel). The ten active (fingers), desirous of performing the ceremony of purification, strain out the same divinity pure, for the exhilarating draught.

5. He who is the fleet god, the omniscient, the lord of praise, when placed by the priests in the vessels, goes by various paths to his holy state through the goat's-hair strainer. This Soma, when pressed, drips down in the holy place for the gods, and enters all their bodies. This immortal god, the slayer of Vritra, the exciter of love in the gods, shines in his own proper seat. He, the rainer of blessings, while uttering a sound as he is pressed by the ten fingers, runs down quickly to the (Drona

Kalaśa) receiving-vessel. He, the purifier, lighted up the Sun, who has his station in the heavens, and the joyful god is placed for the sake of exhilaration in the holy place. He who is the all-enveloping lord, the resounding god, incapable of being injured, is cast by the resplendent Sun (into the holy place).

6. The wise, much-praised god is subjected to bruises in the holy place, and, when purified, he slays all that hate us. He who is the producer of strength, the conqueror of all, is being spread out for Váyu and Indra in the holy place. He who is the head of heaven, the rainer of felicity, the omniscient, expressed Soma, is being carried in consecrated vessels. He who is the lover of the produce of the cow, the desirer of gold, the pure, resplendent god, the conqueror of foes, and himself invincible, utters his voice. He who is the powerful god, the rainer of blessings, the gold-coloured Soma, the purifier, is dripping down pure through the air to meet Indra. He who is the powerful Soma, incapable of sustaining injury, and is the purifier, flows down as the preserver of the gods, and the slayer of the wicked.

7. Soma, the rainer of felicity, when pressed, flows down in the holy place, as the destroyer of Rákshasas, but lover of the gods. He, the all-seeing, gold-coloured, world-sustaining god, is being

distilled in the holy place; and, uttering a sound, he proceeds to the womb of the receiving-vessel. He who is the fleet divinity, the lightener of heaven, the purifier, and slayer of Rákshasas, passing through the goat's-hair strainer, moves forward. He who is our purifier in the celebrated sacrifice of Trita, illuminated the Sun with his rays. Soma, the slayer of Vritra, the rainer of felicity, the bestower of riches, incapable of being injured, moves on like a war-horse. He who is the resplendent and all-wise Soma, when urged forward, moves quickly towards the Drona Kalaśa, to pay his respects to Indra.

8. The man who recites the verses relative to the purifier, containing the essence served up by the Rishis, eats the holy food perfectly pure, which, through the agency of the air, has attained its excellent flavour. The man who, &c., to him Saraswatí, the all-encircling goddess, milks out clarified butter and the sweet moon-plant juice. Let these verses relative to the purifier be the causers of prosperity, the milkers out of precious things, and the distillers of butter. The juice has been served up by the Rishis, and the water of life is by them introduced into us Brahmans. Let these verses relative to the purifying god, when the goddesses are assembled along with the gods, bestow upon us this world and the next, and let them fulfil the

object of our desires. Let these verses relative to the purifying god pour down to us that thousandfold holy stream with which the gods purify our persons. By means of these purifying verses relative to the purifying god, causing prosperity, a man reaches paradise, enjoying by obtaining food the reward of merit, and then goes to the abodes of immortality.

9. We approach with profound reverence that Agni, who shines in his own abode when lighted up, who is ever-young, the glorious illuminator, placed between the heaven and earth, the receiver of many precious oblations, and who manifests himself on every side. Agni, who subdues all our vicious habits by his might, is praised by us as the origin of wealth; let him, when praised by us, preserve us from vice and reproach, and keep uncontaminated our sacrifices. Thou art Varuna (the absolver from guilt), thou art Mitra (our friend to aid in performing acts of merit). O Agni, the sons of Vaśishṫha extol thee with hymns of praise. In thee let all wealth worthy of acceptance reside; and do ye, (O gods,) preserve us at all times with your prospering aids.

10. The mighty Indra increases in might by the praises of Vatsa with the speed of a rainy cloud. When the sons of Kańwa extol Indra, the prosperer of sacrifices, with their songs, then they may pro-

claim vain all the weapons of their foes.[1] While the common priests are eagerly filling the vessels, raising them, and bearing away the produce of the solemn rite, the learned Brahmans serve Indra with a load of praise.

11. The quick-descending, deity-rejoicing streams of the purifying, (darkness)-destroying, gold-coloured, radiance-enveloped juice, are being distilled. The purifier, the mover in fleet chariots, the most brilliant, by his brilliant rays possessed of golden radiance, and accompanied by the Marudgana, (is being distilled.) O purifier, thou who art the bountiful bestower of food, surround us by thy rays, sending to the celebrator of thy praise an illustrious progeny.[2]

12. Sprinkle with water, (ye priests,) from your stations the expressed moon-plant juice, which is the most excellent of all oblations, which, forwarded by men, travels through the midst of the waters, that moon-plant juice which the priests have expressed by the bruising-stones. He who is incapable of sustaining injury, whose smell is most fragrant, when purified, drops down on every side from the goat's-hair strainer. When pressed, we, who mix thee with flour and the produce of the

---

[1] *Or* proclaim the warrior Indra their brother.

[2] *Or* bodily strength.

cow, sing joyous songs to thee, both when raised on high (on the strainer), and when mingled with the waters (in the vessel below). The juicy god, expressed that all may partake of him, the satisfier of the gods, the performer of sacred rites, the brilliant, the all-seeing, flows down.

13. The shining, rain-dispensing, gold-coloured Soma, who, as a king, is worthy of being respectfully approached, has been expressed, and, raising his voice, proceeds to the liquid element (in the vessel below). When purified, thou, O Soma, like a hawk, passest on through the goat's-hair strainer, and takest thy seat on the water-containing receiving-vessel. O possessor of all wisdom, thou goest to the sacred place through love to the sacrifice, and like a horse, when washed, rushing to war, thou rushest to the conflict. Slay our opponents, O Soma, and have compassion on us, when thou overshadowest the waters, and goest to the sacred vessel.

14. As the rays of light encompass the Sun, so do ye with adoration encompass the vast treasure of Indra. Whenever then he is manifested, all wealth will, by his might, be produced; and as the (departed father receives) the portion (offered by the son), so shall we receive that wealth. Praise ye Indra, who gives to the sinless, and is the bestower of wealth: Indra's gifts bring good luck.

He throws his mind into the act of giving, nor will he refuse the petition of him who performs sacrifice.

15. O Indra, give us freedom from the power of those we dread. O possessor of riches, with the aids thou art capable of affording, do thou utterly slay all that hate and rise up against us. O Indra, lord of wealth, thou art in very deed the possessor of large treasures and delightful seats. O god of wealth, object of our praises, we, the pressers of the moon-plant, invoke thee.

16. Thou, O Soma, art (the god) that flows down in a stream, the exhilarating divinity, the most mighty, and one who loves to bestow wealth. Do thou flow down pure in these our solemn rites. Thou, O Soma, when pressed, art full of an exhilarating spirit; thou art the sustainer of the sacrifice; thou art most inebriating, the conqueror of multitudes, and yet thyself invincible. Thou, when bruised by the stones, flowest forth uttering a sound; and bringing us renown-procuring, foe-destroying might.

17. O Soma, flow forth in a stream pure for the banquet of the gods; and, O most delightful god, sit down upon the receiving-vessel. The drops of thy water-seeking, swift-going juice raise in Indra a joyous exhilaration. He and the gods drink thee, the conferrer of pleasure, to obtain immortality.

The pure, expressed, shining liquid, distilling heaven and earth, the all-controlling liquor, forwards wealth to us.

18. They purify by means of the goats' hair the all-desirable, gold-coloured, ash-coloured god, who, himself a god, goes into all the gods by his exhilarating spirit. The ten united, wave-producing fingers wash the renowned bruising-stone, the beloved of Indra. (O Soma), thou art purified for the drinking of Indra, the slayer of Vritra, and that, inspired with vigour, thou mayest bestow gifts upon the man who sits in the hall of oblation.

19. O Soma, flow out pure like a horse washed, and be swift to procure us abundance of strength and wealth. The pressers of the moon-plants purify thy juice. O Soma, purify thy juice for the production of an exhilarating beverage, and for strengthening nourishment. The priests consecrate, by sprinkling, Soma the newly-produced child (of the waters), the gold-coloured, the shining deity, for the benefit of the gods, in the holy place.

20. The gods assemble in presence of the newly-produced Soma, mingling with the waters, who destroys our foes, and is adorned with all becoming ceremonies. Let our voices raise Soma on high, who takes possession of the heart of Indra, as the mother rears her infant. O Soma, object of our sacred hymns, rain down happiness for our herds

of cows, and milk out for us abundance of food, and fill up our reservoirs of water.

21. Those who light up Agni with eagerness, and whose friend is Indra, ever-young, lay down the sacred grass in order, beginning at the east;—whose bundle of fagots is large,[1] whose collection of hymns is extensive, whose club (for warding off intruders) is massy, whose friend is Indra, ever-young;—who in battle subdue by their might the enemies' warriors, whose friend is Indra, ever-young.

22. Indra the supreme, who is but one, and whom no one dares speak against, bestows wealth on the man who offers sacrifice. Whoever among men pressing the moon-plant sits down and attends on the service of the awe-inspiring Indra, to him Indra quickly sends might. Indra in a moment slays the man who will not provide the materials for sacrifice, as one would stamp on a rolled up snake, and at the same moment listens with the utmost attention to our songs of praise.

23. The Sáma Veda singers sing thy praise, the Rig Veda chanters chant to the glorious Indra, and the Yajur Veda officiating priests extol thee, the performer of acts of merit, as (dancers raise high)

---

[1] These are ordered to be of twenty-one pieces, and each piece a cubit long.

the pole (with which they perform their feats).[1] When the institutor of the sacrifice ascends the mountain-top (to pluck the plants), and puts his hand to the solemn rite, then Indra knows his design; and the causer of rain, with his accompanying (Marut) hosts, shakes all things. Then, having yoked his long-maned, girth-expanding, rain-producing horses Harí, Indra, the drinker of the moon-plant beverage, comes to the hearing of our (praise-sounding) voices.

[End of the tenth Adhyáya.]

ELEVENTH ADHYÁYA.

1. O most resplendent Agni, bring the gods to the institutor of this sacrifice, and do thou, as the officiating priest, purify it, and offer up the oblations. O all-wise preserver of the body, forward to-day our most pleasant oblation to the gods for our preservation. I invoke in the present ceremony (Agni), who is extolled by men, the beloved, the sweet-tongued, the offerer of the oblation. O Agni, when extolled by us, bring to us the gods in a most comfortable chariot; for thou art consecrated by men to be the inviter of the gods.

2. Let the faultless Mitra, Aryamá, Savitá, and

[1] *Or* as a good man raises the renown of his family. The ambiguity here is in 'vanśam.'

Bhaga respectively send us at sun-rise whatever (we require). O occupier of excellent abodes, be thou our powerful preserver, when the givers of all gifts come, who take away all our sins. Truly ye, as lords of all, with your mother Aditi, preside over all indestructible rites, and ye, the same lords, possess vast treasures.

3. O thunderbolt-wielding Indra, let our songs delight thee; provide for us food, and utterly slay all who hate the Brahmans. Do thou trample under foot the thievish tribes who offer no sacrifice; for thou art mighty, and like to thee is no one else. Thou, O Indra, art lord of the bruised and unbruised moon-plants; thou art lord of all men.

4. The ever-wakeful, the instructor of the learned priests, Soma the purifier, has taken his seat among the sacrificial ladles; and the oblation-offering priests, in a united band, lay hold on him with their minds bound up in their work, and bringing forward the offering in their propitious hands. He who is the purifier, the supporter of the sacrifice, goes into Indra. He fills both worlds, he destroys darkness. The loved things, sent by him, our beloved, tend to our protection; let him send us wealth, as men support their servants. The increaser of all things, who is himself ever-increasing, the pure Soma, the rainer of felicity,

preserves us by his radiance. Through him our forefathers, who traced the marks (of the stolen cows), and who knew all things, had their minds strongly directed to the hill in which the cows were concealed.

5. O my friends, praise no other being than Indra; why would ye draw on yourselves destruction? Praise Indra, the giver of rain, during the moon-plant sacrifice, and sing his sacred hymns again and again. Praise him, who, like a raging bull or fleet man-subduing heifer, is terrible in his hatred, makes his foes fall down in subjection, both punishes and pardons, is worthy of all reverence, and preserves the animate and inanimate creation.

6. Our most pleasant tuneful voices rise aloft, as the all-conquering, wealth-conveying, indestructible, food-desiring chariots. As the singers, sons of Kańwa, surround the sacred place, and the rays of light the Sun, so do the sons of Bhrigu encompass that all-embracing Indra; and the men who are the sons of Priyamedha adore him with hymns, raising their voices.

7. Do thou with all speed march to the war, and, incapable of being subdued, engage our foes; for it is thou, the destroyer of our debt,[1] that goest to

[1] Probably, the debt of revenge due by us to our foes.

destroy them that hate us. O purifier, thou didst in the watery firmament create the Sun by thy might, and thou movest quickly towards us with a profusion of cows, and enlarged intellects.

8. Do thou with all speed march, &c. (*as before given.*) O thou shining divinity, exhilarating Soma, flow down pure, to grant us immortality, and a happy place of abode. Let Indra drink, O Soma, of thy expressed juice; and let all the other gods drink of it, to obtain intelligence and strength.

9. Like the rays of the Sun, the dripping, exhilarating, newly-produced, new-created, all-diffusing juice flows down on all sides through the stretched out threads, and goes into no other place but into the belly of Indra. The mind of the singer lays hold on him, the sweet juice is sprinkled, the exhilarating liquid produced, and forwarded to the centre of the place where he sits. The purifying, all-expansive, sweet juice of the moon-plant is expressed, and the swift god flows down through the goat's-hair strainer. As when the bull lows, the milch-cow runs towards him, so these divine songs gather around the well-purified vessel of divine moon-plant juice, while Soma presses through the white goat's-hair strainer, and is spread abroad every where, for the production of the protecting liquid, which acts as a coat of mail.

10. O heroes, do ye give birth to Agni by the agency of your fingers, who from the arani-wood falls into the hands of men,[1] and is the illustrious far-seeing lord of families. The priests, who have taken their places, maintain that Agni, pleasant to behold, in his recess, for our preservation from every danger; and he, worthy of adoration and eternal, is ever to be found in his sacred abode. O Agni, ever-young, shine forth with thy swift-ascending flame from thy eastern recess; for thou art a most brilliant god. Let our viands find their way into thy immortal substance.

11. This all-moving radiance proceeds from the east, and takes its seat in mother earth. Afterwards the ever-moving body proceeds to father heaven. Its rays move within man, and from the higher vital air extract and carry down the lower vital air,[2] and the same mighty god enlightens the firmament. The manifestations of the Sun in day and night, by their radiance enlighten the thirty horal mansions, and the voice (of our chanters) sustains the solar manifestations.

[End of the eleventh Adhyáya.]

---

[1] They obtain the fire by rapid friction from the wood, and receive it on cotton, or flax, which they hold in their hands.

[2] *Or* this radiance moves from the heights of heaven to the depths of earth.

TWELFTH ADHYÁYA.

1. We, who approach the faultless sacrifice, chant the sacred liturgy of Agni, who is celebrated by us, even when he is at a distance; that ancient Agni, who rushes on the men that would injure us, and preserves the property of those who offer sacrifice. Let the possessor of all happiness preserve the wealth which we possess, and save us from our sins. Let all living beings celebrate that Agni, who is the slayer of Vritra (the cloud-shaped demon), and who in every battle triumphantly carries off the wealth of the enemy.

2. O shining Agni, yoke those well-trained fleet horses of thine, and let them draw hither thy splendid chariot. Come into our presence, and, regarding the offered viands, bring the gods to the feast, to the moon-plant banquet. O Agni, who layest hold on the sacrifice, possessed of vast brilliance, indestructible, shine forth with thy brilliant all-expansive radiance.

3. Let not the murderous crew hear the dripping sound of the sacrificer's nourishing liquid. Drive away that dog who supplies nothing for the sacrifice, as the sons of Bhrigu drove away (the dog) Makka. The companion of the gods diffuses himself abroad in the holy place as a son leans on his parent's arms (for protection), and quickly

moves to his seat in the sacred receiving-vessel (Yoni), as a gallant proceeds to his paramour, or a husband to his wife. The mighty hero, the furnisher of strength, spreads himself over heaven and earth. The gold-coloured god, as some sacrificer in his own house, moves forward to sit down on the sacred Yoni, in the holy place.

4. O Indra, thou by thy birth art raised above every foe, so constituted that no one can constrain thee; and, without a fellow, yet thou choosest in their wars thy worshippers for thy brotherhood. Thou choosest not to admit to thy friendship the rich miser, nor those drunkards who seek to make havoc. When thou but utterest the inarticulate sound of approbation, then thou bringest (thy wealth) along with thee, and we welcome thee with invitations, as we would (the manes of) a father.

5. Let the hundreds and thousands of long-maned horses, that belong to the all-perfect Indra, be yoked to the golden chariot, and bring him to the moon-plant banquet. Let the peacock-tailed, white-backed pair of horses called Harí, convey thee in a golden chariot to the drinking of the sweet, highly-extolled liquor, and to partake of our viands. O recipient of praise, drink of this well-prepared liquid expressed juice with the eagerness of the (Wind), who first drinks his portion.

This well-expressed pleasant juice is famed for its exhilarating quality.

6. Do ye press and sprinkle on every side with water Soma, fleet as a horse, the object of our praises, the sender of water, the dispenser of radiance, who falls in drops like water, and mingles with the liquid element; who flows down in a thousand streams, is the rainer (of blessings), is expressed like milk, and beloved by all the race of gods. The glorious radiant divinity is produced from water, and increases by water; (press out then) the mighty faithful one.

7. Agni, who desires the sacrificial viands along with hymns of praise, who shines forth, is the brilliant divinity, and the recipient of oblations, destroys darkness, and all our enveloping foes. He also is the all-radiant guardian of father (heaven), resides in the immortal womb of mother (earth), and sits down on the womb of the sacrifice (on the northern *Vedi* or sacred enclosure). O thou who art acquainted with the nature of all beings, and seest all things, bring us food, and progeny, which may be illustrious even in heaven.

8. The glorious divinity, who is purified by the pressure of the gold-ringed fingers,[1] brings his juice

---

[1] There must be four mashas weight of gold made up into rings for each Brahman who presses the moon-plants. These rings are not rounded, but flattened like a new cart-wheel ring.

in contact with the gods, and, when pressed, moves all over the sacred strainer, uttering a sound like that of the invoker of the gods, when he goes to the newly-constructed house where an animal is bound for sacrifice. Do thou, the mighty one, clad in warlike apparel, the far-seeing god, the extoller of those who again and again celebrate thy praise, the purifier, the surveyor of all things, the ever-wakeful divinity, enter between the bruising planks for this divine banquet. The most famed amid the famed, he who extends over all the earth, the beloved, who is raised on the goat's-hair strainer, is being purified for us. O sustainer and purifier, utter on every side thy voice, and ever preserve us by thy saving aids.

9. Let us praise quickly the ever-prosperous Indra, who has been purified (from the stain of the murder of the Rákshasas) by the purifying psalmody and by the purifying liturgical hymns.[1] Let now Soma, who sustains all purifying substances, become his delight. O purified Indra, come to us thyself purified, with thy purified assistant Maruts. O purified drinker of the moon-plant beverage, establish us in the possession of wealth, and, when purified, enjoy the inebriating

---

[1] These two phrases refer respectively to the hymns of the Rig and Sáma Vedas.

juice. O Indra, when purified, thou bestowest on us wealth; when purified, thou givest the institutor of the sacrifice his reward; when purified, thou slayest our foes, and lovest to send us food.

10. We, who desire the sacrificial articles, and who lay hold on heaven, sing the merit-conferring psalter of the resplendent Agni. Agni is the forwarder of sacrifices performed in the world of man; let him accept our songs, and let him convey the sacrifice to the family of the gods. Thou, O Agni, growest great on all sides, art our beloved one, and worthy of all praise; for by thy aid the sacrifice is rendered complete in all its parts.

11. The voices of the priests are employed in praising him, who is worshipped in the three daily sacrifices, is the rainer of felicity, is the giver of food, and the loud-sounding divinity. Spreading over the waters (in the receiving-vessel), as Varuna does over the sea, he bestows most desirable jewels. Do thou flow out pure, who art surrounded by the brave and attended by heroes, art the subduer, the conqueror, the receiver of wealth, the holder of sharp weapons, invincible in war, and ever overthrowing thy enemies in battle. O performer of immense journeys, who procurest security for thy worshippers, and makest heaven and earth happy, drop down pure, thou who lovest to meet the waters at the early dawn, when the Sun is in the

meridian, and when the solar rays are departing, and summonest for us strengthening food.

12. O preserver of strength, when thou art joined to the holy Soma thou art most illustrious. Thou, the invincible, the sustainer of men by thyself alone, slayest the indomitable Rákshasas. We beg wealth of thee at the present time, of thee at all times, as the manes beg their allotted portion. Thy mansions in the heavens, O Indra, are as far extended as the voice of fame. Let floods of happiness from thee compass us around.

13. We worship the deity who, even among the gods, is worthy of adoration, the inviter of the gods, the immortal, the carrier on of the sacrifice to perfection; the preserver of liquids,[1] possessor of brilliant treasures, the all-resplendent Agni, encompassed with surpassing radiance. Let him offer up the liquor that imparts delight to Mitra and Varuna, in the shining oblation-hall.[2]

14. O Agni, let unfailing stores of provisions come to the men whom thou protectest in the conflict and sendest to the wars. O destroyer of foes, nothing, not even the least thing, belonging to such a man, can be carried off, and his strength is every where famous. Let the lord of all men

---

[1] *Or* grandson of liquids, 'napátam,' *nepotem*. See Ad. xv. 5.

[2] *Or* shining heavens.

be our preserver in the wars through means of troops of horses, and let him become the bestower of all valuable things through means of the sacrifices of our learned Brahmans.

15. When the ten united, purifying, sustaining sisters (the fingers) propel the mighty Soma, the gold-coloured drippings flow down like the rays of the Sun, and spread themselves abroad in the receiving-vessel with the speed of a fleet horse. The deity-desiring, happiness-raining, much-praised moon-plant juice is laid hold of by the sacred waters, as the child is by the mother, and runs towards its prepared seat in the receiving-vessel, along with the produce of the cow, with the eagerness a man does towards a woman. Truly Soma has drunk from the udder of the indestructible cow, and, himself of surpassing intellect, flows down in many streams into one receptacle; and the cows envelope the supreme divinity with their milk, as it were with newly-washed garments.

16. O Indra, drink to thy satisfaction of our savoury pressed juice, mingled with the product of the cow. And when thou hast drunk, and art under the influence of the liquor, acknowledge us by granting us prosperity, and let thy favourable regards protect us. May we, the providers of sacrificial food, be kept in a good frame of mind, and not be left a prey to our foes; preserve thou us

with all thy wondrous aids, and keep us ever in peace.

17. The twenty-one milch-cows[1] yield to him the true milk, in the superexcellent place of sacrifice;[2] and the four delightful liquids are produced for the purifying of men as often as they are brought to perfection in the sacrifice. The two worlds are borne aloft by the hymns in praise of the purified delightful water of life;[3] and Soma with his might encircles the shining waters, whenever the preparers of the sacred viands enter the mansion of the radiant god. Let the exciting, immortal, inextinguishable rays of light tend to the preservation of the inhabitants of the two worlds, and with them let Soma send down pure, strengthening, divine nourishment, and afterwards let hymns of praise rise to the resplendent king.

18. Do thou, the much-extolled, the purifier, approach for the banquet of Váyu, of Mitra, of Varuna, and the hero Indra, who is fleet as thought, stands in a chariot, is the producer of rain, and the wielder of the thunderbolt. O divine Soma, favour us with garments to cover us well, and with pure

---

[1] Most probably metres; *or* the twelve months, five seasons, three worlds, and one Sun.

[2] *Or* in the lofty heavens.

[3] *Aqua vitæ*. The other three liquids may be water, milk, and melted butter.

milch-cows, and with joy-bringing golden ornaments, and with horses fit for the chariot. O purifier, rain down upon us all kinds of heavenly and earthly wealth; and through means of thee, may we gain possession of wealth worthy of Rishis, and such as was possessed by Jamadagni.

19. O unequalled proprietor, who wast produced for the destruction of the Rákshasas, thou at one and the same time renderest habitable the earth, and raisest up the pillars of heaven. On thy account sacrifices were instituted, and the joy-causing hymns composed. Thou art the creator of all things that have been or are to be. Do thou, who elevatedst the Sun in the heavens, infuse fertility into our milch-cows. And do ye, our priests, warm the heart of Indra, the recipient of praise, with the well-polished hymns of the grand Sáma, as others do with the affecting verses of the common Sáma.

20. As the adorable Soma, the causer of inebriating delight, flows into the vessel, do thou, O possessor of the horses Harí, drink and be merry. The rainer (of blessings), the shining Soma, the nourisher, the giver of thousands of gifts, is being prepared for the sender down of rain. O Indra, let the exciting, blessing-conferring, exhilarating, extolled, aiding, adored, foe-destroying, immortality-conferring draughts reach us. Thou art brave, thou art the giver of gifts; send us therefore the chariot

of mankind (sacrifice) to convey us to heaven. At the same time, all-subduing god, do thou burn up, as thou wouldst a wooden vessel, the wretch who neglects sacred rites.

[End of the twelfth Adhyáya.]

THIRTEENTH ADHYÁYA.

1. O Soma, pour forth to us rain, even floods of water on all sides, in abundance, and large supplies of wholesome food. O Soma, flow forth in such a stream that the cows of the men (who are hostile to us) may come to our houses. O most beloved of the gods, do thou in this sacrifice pour forth to us water in a stream; pour forth abundant showers of rain. Let (Soma) furnish us, in a full stream, with the pure liquid strained through the goats' hair, for consumption; and let the gods hear the sound of his approach. The purifier, slaying the Rákshasas, and, as of old, shedding rays of radiance, comes down in showers.

2. O priests, bring forth the liquor for the god Indra, who delights in quaffing it, who knows all things, who moves around on every side, who comes to attend at the sacrifice, and moves forward at the head of the divinities. Do ye approach the drinker of the moon-plant beverage, the foe-subduing Indra, with vessels full of expressed, shining

moon-plant juice. When the priests approach Indra with the bowls of shining moon-plant juice, the knower of all things, the attendant on sacrifices, the seizer of our enemies, sends whatever we desire. For him, even for him, O ye priests, bring the expressed nourishing liquid, that we may never by any accident suffer the misery of subjugation to any of those our opponents who seek to subdue us.

3. O sing a song to the yellow, rose-coloured Soma, who subsists by his own might, and touches the heavens. Purify the Soma juice expressed by the hand-impressed stones, and pour the sweet milk into the sweet spirit. Sit down to sing hymns of praise, mingle the moon-plant juice with the curdled milk, and introduce the sparkling liquor into the person of Indra. O Soma, who providest for the gods the object of their desire, slayer of our foes, the all-seeing, pour down felicity for our cattle. O Soma, searcher of the heart, lord of the mind, thou art poured out for Indra for his drinking and exhilaration. O sparkling, purifying Soma, do thou, along with Indra, confer on us wealth, accompanied with bodily vigour.

4. O mighty divinity, thou ever bringest with thee wealth well worthy of notice, art the rainer of felicity, the refuge of man, the fountain of beneficence. Let the invincible slayer of Vritra, who overthrew by the might of his arm ninety-nine

cities (for Divodása), bestow on us wealth. Let Indra, our friend, the conferrer of happiness, milk out as it were for us in a full stream (the riches) which consist in horses, cows, and barley.[1]

5. Let the glorious (solar) luminary drink the powerful spirit of the moon-plant liquor, and bestow upon the institutor of this sacrifice a life free from adversity. The luminary that is moved round by the aerial vortex, that preserves the world by its own might, and that nourishes all its inhabitants, and pours forth floods of light; the glorious, mighty, all-embracing, food-producing, unfading luminary, placed on the ground of the heaven-sustaining circle,[2] the destroyer of the unfriendly, the slayer of foes, the exterminator of the injurious, the destroyer of the Asurs, and the slayer of our envious kindred, has been manifested. The all-surpassing, most excellent light of lights, all-conquering, and wealth-procuring, is termed the Mighty Radiance. The glorious, radiant, mighty Sun sheds abroad his attendant, mighty, indestructible influence, to give light to the world.

---

[1] Observe here the principal articles of rural wealth at the time and place when these hymns were written. There is no mention of buffaloes, rice, or wheat, so common now in India.

[2] The reader must turn to the Ptolemaic astronomy here for an object of comparison. But the Hindu writers seem actually to have thought of a material circle.

6. O Indra, help forward our sacred rites, bestow on us wealth with the readiness a father bestows it on his son. O thou, who art much extolled in this sacrifice, grant that we living creatures may daily see the light of the Sun. O brave hero, let not the ignorant, murderous, knavish bands run us down, since we perform propitious rites. When also we embark in boats, may we pass safely over many waters through thy aid.

7. O Indra, save us day by day, to-morrow after to-morrow, and ever and anon. As thou, O protector of holy men, daily preservest the singers of thy praise, so preserve thou us by night and by day. O brave hero, destroyer of foes, god of riches, and laden with wealth, who mixest the juice that produces vigour, performer of many meritorious acts, and rainer down of felicity, let both thy hands lay hold on the (Vajra) thunderbolt.

8. We, desirous of wives, and desirous of sons, ever first to move to the sacrifice, the givers of distinguished gifts, invoke (Saraswán) the god Oceanus. Also let (Śaraswatí) the river goddess, beloved above beloveds by the seven-fold sisterhood,[1] the much-extolled goddess, be praised by us.

9. We meditate on the adorable light of the

---

[1] The seven rivers; *or* the seven musical cadences.

divine parent. Let him direct our understandings. *Or*, we are sustained by the superexcellent provisions, furnished us by the resplendent Sun. May he prosper our sacred rites.[1]

[*Sománam—given before*].

10. [*Agna ayú—before. Tanah shaktan—before.*] O Mitra and Varuna, twin gods, who are without hate and always prospering, do ye encompass the much-desired, mighty performers of sacrifice for the purpose of obtaining water.

11. O ye who dwell in the rainy skies, who cause the waters to flow down, ye who are the lords of food, famed for liberality, do ye ascend your mighty chariot. The inhabitants of the three worlds bind, by their sacred rites, (Indra in the form of) the Sun, Fire, and Wind. The stars also that shine in the heavens (are but forms of Indra).[2]

12. These beloved, well-paired, powerful, hero-conveying, bay horses Harí are being yoked to the chariot. O hero, thou art every day manifested with the rays of the morning, imparting life to the torpid, and giving form to the shapeless masses of beings.

13. O Indra, this moon-plant beverage is expressed for thee, and for thee is strained out pure;

---

[1] These are two translations of the famous Gáyatri. The latter is most probably the nearer to its original meaning.

[2] In these bold additions I have but followed the Bháshya.

therefore do thou drink of it. It is thou that formest the shining moon-plant, which moves with a horse's fleetness, and thou that overshadowest it, that it may produce the strengthening, exhilarating draught. He, the mighty god, like a chariot conveying large treasures, brings them to confer them on us. At such a time let all the works produced by men, which tend to exaltation, meet in the awful heaven-conferring conflict.[1] O conferrer of strength, strain out for us strength like that of the Maruts, like that of the spotless heavenly hosts, or like that of waters rushing rapidly. Become to us the purifier of the mind, O thou who art manifested in a thousand streams, and deemed worthy of receiving a share in the sacrifice, as well as the subduer of armies.

14. Thou, O Agni, hast been consecrated by the gods to be the oblative priest for all the sacrifices performed in the world of human beings. Thou satisfiest with our exhilarating oblations the objects of our adoration through the medium of thy (flaming) tongue. Thou both conveyest the gods to us, and presentest our offering to them. O Agni, thou art the institutor and carrier on to perfection of all merit-conferring rites. Thou art in-

---

[1] The conflict 'vája' (or 'bája') is either a sacrifice or a battle, as the Hebrew לחם means 'bread,' or 'a battle.'

timately acquainted with all the roads and paths of sacrificial rites; therefore (do thou conduct us through them).

15. The offerer of oblations, the gift-conferring, the immortal (Agni), who leads by his practical wisdom into the knowledge of all objects of science, presents himself at the very commencement of our ceremonies. This powerful warrior is the subject of meditation in our wars; and in our sacrifices is first put in his sacred recess, and then, as officiating priest, is the provider of all the materials of sacrifice. Established by our consecratory rites, (Agni,) the object of our adoration, sustains the womb of Being; and the daughter of Daksha (the consecrated ground) sustains him, her protecting father.

16. Do ye sprinkle the clarified butter mixed with milk on (Agni) the supporter of heaven and earth; and lay hold (of the gifts) of the rainer of felicity in the midst (of his pleasant feast). As cows know to go to their own homes, as calves follow along with their mothers, and as sisters go paired with their brothers, so all the sacrificial viands preparing for consumption proceed through the air to Indra and Agni, and are about to fall into the jaws of the all-consuming deity.

17. That primeval (essence alone) has in itself a real existence amid all worlds. From it the all-

inspiring radiant Sun[1] was produced. He, when he manifests himself, destroys our foes, and all creatures find joy in reposing in him. He who increases in might, is of great strength, and the slaughterer (of the wicked), inspires fear into his slavish (foes). He also is the purifier of all animate and inanimate creatures. When in thy merry moods, all the creation thou upholdest seek a refuge in thee. All the satisfiers of the gods with sacrifices cause their works to centre in thee; therefore they become double and triple (by obtaining wives and sons). Create, O Indra, through pleasure, an (heir) pleasanter than all pleasant things. Also, when greatly exhilarated, do thou sport for us through sweetness a sweet (babe).[2]

18. O venerable, might-possessing, self-satisfying Indra, do thou drink to the full extent of thy desire, along with Vishnu, the moon-plant juice mixed with barley, on the Trikadra days. It was the mighty Soma truly that raised the spirits of the all-glorious Indra for the performance of his mighty work, the slaying of Vritra. May he, that same faithful Indu, now surround that same divine faithful Indra. O Indra, thou wast born endued

---

[1] The Bháshya says 'Súrya' means here Indra.

[2] The Bh. adds 'mithuna,' but I prefer the obscurity of the original.

with merit, and by thy might thou carriest round the world; thou art powerful by thy inherent power, thou art great in might; thou art the subduer of foes, the omniscient god, possessed of much wisdom, the bestower of the much-desired wealth on the celebrators of thy praise. May the same divine faithful Indu (Soma) encompass all around that same faithful Indra. Afterwards the brilliant Indra by his might slew in war Kravi, and again rendered prosperous heaven and earth, after (that Rákshas) had filled them by his power. Indra receives into his own belly one-half (of the moon-plant beverage) and sends the other to the gods. May the same divine faithful Indu encompass the same faithful Indra.

[End of the thirteenth Adhyáya.]

FOURTEENTH ADHYÁYA.

1. Celebrate, in songs of praise with the greatest attention, Indra the lord of cattle; for he is capable of appreciating your services, is the son of the sacrifice,[1] and the preserver of holy men. Let the gold-coloured shining horses of Indra present themselves on the sacred grass, where we are praising Indra. The cows let down their sweet milk to be

[1] On account of the love he bears it.—Bh.

mingled with the moon-plant juice, for Indra the holder of the thunderbolt, when the liquor is brought from all sides into his presence.

2. Do ye set in elegant array our sacrificial viands, and the liquors for the sacrifice, before the oblation-receiving Indra, in every contest in which he is engaged. O slayer of Vritra, most excellent handler of the bow-string, who art made propitious by praise, (fulfil our desires.) Thou art the principal giver of wealth, the all-faithful, the possessor of celebrity; we therefore ask what becomes the majesty of the possessor of abundant treasures, and the son of mighty strength.

3. The heavenly inhabitants milk out of the mighty firmament the ancient liquor praised in by-gone ages, and with their eyes turned to Indra extol the newly-produced (juice). Afterwards those divine all-seeing Vasurach praise their relation (Soma) before the shining Sun has dispelled the darkness. And thou, O purifying Soma, becomest the ornament of heaven and earth, and of all creatures, through thy glorious might, as a bull is of the herd of cattle amid which he is stationed.

4. Agni, do thou without fail repeat among the gods this our oblation-accompanying new hymn of praise, proclaimed near thy eastern recess.[1] O

---

[1] The Áhavaníya Kunda.—Bh.

Agni, possessed of varied splendour, thou art the distributor of wealth; and as a wave of the sea opposite to the mouth of a river sends into it a portion of its waters, so now thou rainest happiness on the institutor of a sacrifice. Do thou dispense to us provisions from the highest heavens and from the regions of mid-air, and bestow on us the wealth of this lower world.

5. I am the person who in verity lay hold of the intellect of the preserver of sacrifices; I have an origin resplendent as that of the Sun. Born like Kańwa in ancient days, I adorn Indra with my songs of praise, excited by which he puts on his mighty strength. There are those who make no effort to please thee, and there were Rishis who pleased thee perfectly; do thou, when fully praised by me, (who belong to neither class,) manifest all thy greatness.

6. O Agni, do thou with all thy attendant fires accept of our strength-conferring oblations, and with all the fires which exist among gods and men, favourably receive our hymns of praise. May that Agni, to whom the priests make oblations, with all his attendant fires come into our presence, surrounded with stores of provisions for ourselves, our sons, and our grandsons. Do thou, O Agni, with all thy attendant fires raise aloft our hymns of praise, as well as our sacrifices. Do thou send

us (virtuous men), for the offering of libations to the gods, and conferring on us wealth.

7. O primeval Soma, that sittest on the matting of cut Kuśa grass, the sacrificers inspire thee with a mind to bestow large stores of food and might. O hero, inspire us with heroism. Thou art cut for the sacrificial nourishing beverage, like some inexhaustible reservoir of water, or like water by the fingers of the hand of him that lifts it. O immortal (Soma), thou becomest for mortals the Sun in the firmament that supports the immortal, genuine, heart-rejoicing waters, and thou continually waitest on the sacrifice-honouring gods with reference to our wars.

8. Distil the sparkling liquor for Indra, let him drink of the sweet moon-plant essence; for it is he who by his might sends you wealth. I celebrate the lord of the horses Harí, the giver of wealth; let him now hear the praise of the son of Aśwa who extols him. O thou primeval god, no one was ever produced equal to thee in heroism, no one is comparable to thee for wealth, nor for affording protection, nor for graciously accepting our songs of praise.

9. Thou, (O my host,) desirest the produce of the cow; therefore (I call on) the producer of the morning rays, who causes the waters to resound when they mingle together, the protector of (the cow), the animal it is criminal to injure.

10. Let the divine (Agni), the giver of wealth, desire the long ladle (*śruk*) with its full liquid oblation. Pour ye out, fill ye up; for in very deed the divine (Agni) bears you up. The gods constituted the intellect-conferring Agni, the inviter to sacrifices, and bearer away of oblations. Agni gives jewels, accompanied with heroes, to the man who offers sacrifice according to the instituted mode.

11. Let Agni, who knows all the roads, in whom all sacred rites centre, manifest himself; and let our songs find their way to Agni, propitiously brought into being, and the prosperer of men of priestly families. Since mortals tremble at the performers of sacred rites, do ye in this sacrifice worship with oblations, with all your (powers), Agni the giver of thousands of gifts. Agni, when hailed by Divodása with his mighty voice, did not leave the gods to wander about mother earth, but (collecting them) brilliant and glorious left his house in the heavens.

12. *Agna Ayuńsi*—[*as before*]. We, the five tribes,[1] call upon Agni who is extolled by the mighty gods; for Agni is all-seeing, is the purifier, the protector of the five tribes, and the first

---

[1] The four castes, and the still more degraded tribe of Parwárís; *or* Gandharvas, Pitaras, Devas, Asuras, and Rákshasas; *or* gods, men, Gandharvas, Apsaras, and serpents.

consecrated, and put in his sacred recess. O Agni, performer of holy acts, pour out for us glory accompanied with might, and give us wealth and provisions.

13. O purifying, shining Agni, with thy brilliant exhilarating tongue bring hither the gods, and impart to them the oblation. O thou who art fed by melted butter, and art possessed of surpassing radiance, we desire thy presence, for thou art the observer of all things. Bring thou the gods to the banquet. O all-wise Agni, we light up in this sacrifice thee, who delightest in oblations, and art a resplendent mighty divinity.

14. O Agni, the object of our adoration in all sacred rites, into whom the continued flow of hymned verses enters, save us by thy protecting aids. Save us, O Agni, bring us wealth, the destroyer of poverty, worthy of being extolled, and which can never be taken from us by foes in any war. O Agni, bring to us for our sustenance heart-delighting wealth, the producer of happiness, and which will last all our lives.

15. Our sacred rites urge forward Agni (to the sacrifice), as (horsemen) a fleet horse into the wars. Through him may we acquire by conquest every species of wealth. O Agni, send us such sufficient aid from thee, as thereby we may obtain herds of cows; furnish us also with thy aid for the acquisi-

tion of wealth. O Agni, bring from heaven great and ever-increasing wealth, accompanied with horses and cows; illuminate the heavens, and fight against our foes. O Agni, thou causedst the ever-moving, immortal Sun to take his place aloft in the heavens, that he might give light to the sons of men. O Agni, thou art the enlightener of all, the most beloved, who sittest chief at our (sacrifices). Honour with thy regard (our hymns), and supply the singers with food.

16. O Agni, thou art the head of the gods, overtopping the heavens, resembling the eminence on a bullock's shoulders; the lord of earth, the inspirer of delight into all animate and inanimate beings. O Agni, lord of heaven, thou art the lord of wealth, worthy of being praised and of being bestowed. It is thou that bestowest happiness; let me then be the celebrator of thy praise, O Agni; thy pure, white, shining rays urge onwards thy brilliant flames.

[End of the fourteenth Adhyáya.]

FIFTEENTH ADHYÁYA.

1. Who, among men, O Agni, is worthy of being reckoned thy brother? for who else can acceptably offer thee sacrifice? Who knows thy essence, or where thy secret abode is? Thou, O Agni, art

the brother, the friend, the beloved of us men. Thou as a friend art worthy of being praised by our friends. Offer thou up our oblations to Mitra and Varuna; offer to the rest of the gods the great sacrifice, and for this purpose proceed to thy own sacred recess.

2. He who is worthy of all praise and of being adored by all, the foe of darkness, who is to be reverently approached, the rainer of felicity, now shines forth. Agni, the rainer of happiness, who like some horse conveys to us the gods, now shines forth; him the offerers of sacrifice praise. O rainer of felicity, we, the rainers down of offerings, make thee, the causer of rain, the brilliant Agni, to shine forth.

3 O radiant Agni, thy mighty, brilliant, white rays proceed upwards. O much-desired Agni, let our long-scooped ladles, holding melted butter, enter thee, and honour with acceptance our oblations. I praise Agni, the exhilarator, the inviter (of the gods), the receiver of the offerings, who is possessed of varied radiance and brilliant treasures: let him listen to our song.

4. Save us, O Agni, by one sacred song; save us also by two. O lord of food, save us by three. O appointer of our place of abode, save us by four. Save us, O Agni, from every miserly Rákshas; protect us in our battles, for we surround thee,

who art always most near to us and our brothers, to aid us in our oblations to the gods, and to promote our prosperity.

5. Thou, O brilliant king, art regarded as lord, as the only one who has access to the gods, as the radiant divinity, the terrifier of foes, to procure the prosperity of thy worshippers, and of illustrious birth. The possessor of all knowledge comes while it is yet night, displaying his white radiance. When he subdues the black retiring (night) with his radiance, bringing to light the virgin daughter of the mighty protecting luminary, he then moves along with his heaven-enveloping rays, and shines forth, planting on high the solar radiance. The prosperous venerable Agni comes to promote our prosperity, and afterwards, as the destroyer (of darkness), goes to his sister's abode. Agni, standing forth with his enlivening heavenly beams and white-coloured rays, opposes the nocturnal darkness.

6. O Agni, son of fuel, and great-grandson of sacrificial food,[1] with what hymns shall we fully praise thee, the famed destroyer of foes? O son of strength,[2] what kind of divinity-revering offerings

---

[1] This genealogy is thus reckoned in the Bháshya. Oblations procure rain; rain nourishes trees; from wood, Agni or fire is procured by friction.

[2] *i. e.* produced by the strong arms of the priests.

shall we present, when we offer up this hymn of adoration? Do thou afterwards cause all our hymns of praise to procure for us desirable places of abode, and food united with wealth.

7. O Agni, come with thy attendant fires; for we long for thee, the inviter (of the gods). Let the oblation held (by the priests) sprinkle thee, the object of our worship, on thy seat on the sacred grass. O son of strength, descendant of Angiras, the long ladles run to thee during the sacrifice; and we pray to Agni, the great-grandson of food, possessor of shining hair, all-sufficient during the sacred rites.

8. Let our hymns of praise come before the god possessed of consuming radiance, worthy of being respectfully approached, and let our sacrifices, offered with adoration, enter thee, the possessor of much wealth, and the object of many hymns of praise for our protection. We pray to Agni, the son of strength, the parent of wealth, that he may give us all valuable possessions; to him, who appears in a double character, as an immortal god, and among men as a highly-excited performer of sacrifice amid the priests.

9. Agni, who is the leader of all the tribes of men (in the paths of religion), who is quick (to aid his worshippers), and like a chariot (to carry away the offerings), and always produced anew (from the

araṅi-wood), is incapable of being slain by any one. The man who offers sacrifice obtains food by means of the bearer away (of oblations), and a place of abode from the god possessed of pure radiance. Agni, the subduer of all our leagued foes, and the nourisher of the immortal gods, is possessed of immense stores of provisions.

10. Let Agni, when he receives provisions, be propitious to us; let our gift be propitious, let our sacrifice be propitious, and our hymns of praise be propitious. Make our mind propitious amid the assault of our foes, so that thou mayest by us conquer in war. Subdue the many firm bands of our opponents, since we worship thee to obtain the object of our desires.

11. O Agni, son of strength, parent of wealth, lord of provisions conjoined with cows, give to us abundance of food. He, the resplendent divinity, the assigner to us of a place of abode, the all-wise, the god celebrated by our voices, accompanied by many delight-inspiring flames, shines forth to us, as the conferrer of provisions accompanied with wealth. O resplendent Agni, cast down (the Rákshasas by thy auxiliaries) in union with thy own might, and do thou with thy fiery mouth burn them up one by one.

12. All men who desire food (adore) the much-loved Agni, our beloved guest: I too, for the ob-

taining of felicity, employ my voice in praising Agni with hymns, who has been set up in your house. The men who offer sacrifices extol in hymns of praise him who offers the clarified butter to the gods, as they would to a friend. We praise Agni the parent of wealth, who lauds (the institutor of sacrifices), and who in these solemnities sends forward to heaven the prepared offerings.

13. I praise in this sacrifice with an enkindling voice the enkindled Agni. I urge forward him who is himself pure and the purifier of others, and stable as the pole. I worship with delight-inspiring hymns the possessor of wisdom, the inviter of the gods, who is extolled by multitudes, and without malice; the all-wise god, who is intimately acquainted with every living creature. O Agni, gods and men have consecrated thee age after age, thee as the herald of the gods, the immortal, the offerer of oblations, the preserver, the god who ought to be extolled, and have worshipped thee as the ever-wakeful, the all-pervading, and the lord of men. O Agni, who renderest glorious both worlds during the performance of our rites, thou goest backwards and forwards through the two worlds as the messenger of the gods: since, therefore, we apply ourselves to sacred rites and sacred hymns, be thou manifested as the prosperer of these three habitable regions (of earth, air, and heaven).

14. Our sister voices, raised for the benefit of the offerer, celebrating thy perfections, rise in thy presence, whilst thou art blown up by the wind. The (aerial) waters touch the seat of him who sits on the three-jointed sacred grass, first bound and then loosed. The seat of the resplendent rainer of felicity is to be religiously guarded by our friendly protection, and the appearance of Agni is to be adored with the same reverence as the Sun.

[End of the fifteenth Adhyáya.]

SIXTEENTH ADHYÁYA.

1. O Indra, mortal men invite thee with their hymns to come to receive the first draught of the moon-plant liquor. The united Ribhus celebrate thee, and the Rudras sing to thee, the primeval divinity. Indra increases the staminal vigour of the institutor of this sacrifice, through the drinking of the expressed juice, so that his whole frame being exhilarated, men praise the might of Indra now as they did in former days.

2. The hymning, singing priests, skilled in sacred song, worship Indra and Agni. I, too, extol them to obtain provisions. O Indra and Agni, do ye suddenly by one blow overthrow the ninety slavish foe-protecting cities. O Indra and Agni, the priests who lay hold of the moon-plant juice by way of

oblation employ themselves in our solemn rites. O Indra and Agni, strength and food which mutually produce one another are with you, and in you also are stored up supplies of water.

3. O Indra, husband of Śachi, come with all thy auxiliary (Maruts) to bestow on us the object of our desire; for, O mighty hero, we worship thee, that renowned divinity, who in bestowing is equal to Fortune. O divinity, it is thou that satisfiest us with horses, and bestowest on us abundance of cows; thou art the golden, the joyous divinity. With thee there is no lack of gifts; bring to us whatever we ask.

4. Do in very deed come for the benefit of our children, and possess thyself of wealth to bestow on us pecuniary aid. O Indra, possessor of wealth, rain down on us who desire cows, and on us who desire horses, (the objects of our desire.) O Indra, thou bestowest on the institutors of sacrifice many hundreds and thousands of herds of cattle. We, who sing at the top of our voices thy praises to procure thy aid, bring thee, the destroyer of cities, into our presence.

5. The inviter of the gods, the joyful Agni, is the bestower of all the wealth that men possess. As the first goblets of moon-plant liquor are drunk up by him, so let the same Agni drink in our praise. O lord of all, worthy of being reverently

approached, the bestowers of oblations who desire the favour of the gods adorn thee with praises, as men would adorn a chariot-horse. Rain down then both on our sons and grandsons the wealth of the wealthy.

6. O Varuna, hear this my invitation, and have mercy on me; for I, desirous of thy aid, especially address thee. O rainer of felicity, what is thy preserving march with which thou comest to make us joyful? and what is that with which thou comest, bringing gifts to him who chants thy praise?

7. We, his worshippers, call upon Indra to the banquet of the gods, on Indra while the sacrifice is providing, and on Indra when it is terminating. We call on Indra to bestow on us wealth. Indra, by the greatness of his might, stretched out the heavens and the earth, and made the Sun ascend to his place. In Indra all beings centre, and the goblets of moon-plant liquor find in him a place.

8. (O Viśwakarma[1]), creator of all things, who didst arrive at thy elevation through the performance of sacrifice, do thou in my person perform the service of this consecrated (Agni). Let all other men befool themselves, but let Indra be present with us, as the bestower of riches, and the conductor to heaven.

---

[1] It may be questioned whether Viśwakarma be not rather an epithet of Indra than the god of that name.

9. (Soma) the purifier, by his gold-coloured sparkling stream and accompanying rays, destroys all who hate us, as the Sun by his beams (the hateful darkness). The stream of the sprinkled moon-plant is all-luminous; and the gold-coloured purifier, who with his extolled sevenfold mouth and rays encompasses all the starry bodies, becomes radiant. The knowing Soma moves to the glorious eastern region; and his divine, reverently-to-be-approached chariot comes along with the solar rays, even his reverently-to-be-approached chariot. The sacred hymns uttered by men come up to Indra, and rejoice the conqueror; and the thunderbolt at the same time comes to his hand. Be ye then, (Soma and Indra,) invincible in the battle, ever invincible.

10. It was thou, O Soma, who in reality found out the treasure concealed by the Pañi,[1] by means of the supporting maternal waters used to aid in the sacrifice, in thy own abode, even in thy own abode. As the voice of the singer of the Sáma is heard at a great distance, so is the sound of the bruising-stones, in which those that lay hold of them greatly delight. Meanwhile the brilliant Soma with his three-world-sustaining shining rays sends us food,—yes, sends us food.

---

[1] It was Indra properly who found the cows, the treasure here alluded to; but he had drunk the Soma juice, or he could not have performed that feat.

11. Confer on us for our preservation an intellect for obtaining cows, horses, food, and heroes.

12. O (Maruts), heroes possessed of substantial might, grant his desire to the hymning, sweating, moving chanter.

13. May the sons of immortality hear our songs and be propitious to us.

14. We cause our high praises to centre in your brilliant heavens and earth, and approach for the purpose of praising your pure (divinity). Ye two, with your persons, and also with your might, purify both the sacrifice and sacrificer, and even offer up the oblation; ye, the mighty ones, furnish our friend (the singer with what he desires). Ye preserve and supply food, and are the support of the sacrifice.

15. (O Indra), this (moon-plant juice) is for thee, and thou approachest it as the pigeon does his mate. On account of it, also, thou regardest our songs of praise. O hero, lord of wealth, who art extolled by our voices, whose fame is as we have celebrated it, thy magnificence and thy glory combine excellence with substantialness. O performer of many merit-conferring acts, stand over us for our preservation in this conflict; at the same time we seek thy counsel in all our affairs.

16. Ye givers of milk, approach the mighty hero (Indra); for during the sacrifice the reward-con-

ferring (cow and goat's milk) are to be furnished in abundance to the god, both of whose ears are adorned with golden ear-rings. The (sacrifice-) bearing (priests) have proceeded to pour forth in abundance the sweet liquor into the large vessel, at the ceremony of taking leave of the personified oblation. Bowing reverently, sprinkle the personified oblation,[1] with the circle on its forehead, and its door below, and which is all-diffusive and imperishable.

17. Let us, through thy friendship, live void of fear and free from pain, and let us see the mighty foe-destroying work of thine exhibited as it was to Turvaśa and Yada. O rainer of felicity, thou overshadowest all the sacrifice-performing division of the world, and no hewer down of warriors can injure thee.[2] The pleasant milk-yielding (moon-plants), rivalling the honey-bee, are being sprinkled with water; come quickly, make haste, and drink their juice.

18. Let these songs of mine, (O Indra,) possessor of much wealth, magnify thee; while our pure, learned priests, glorious as the brilliant flame, celebrate thee in hymns of praise. He, having his might increased by the songs of a thousand Rishis,

---

[1] This is barley-meal, &c., made up in the form of a man's head, which is marked and worshipped as described in the text.

[2] *Or*, he is never angry with him who offers oblations.

swells out like the sea, and the same ever-propitious divinity has his might and strength celebrated during the sacrifice by the glorious Brahmanical psalmody.

19. This treasure-guarding sacrifice of thine redounds to the benefit of all, both of lord and slave; and the sacrificial thing which is brought forth for thee existed before (as a mental conception) in the all-controlling lord (Brahmá), the father of Saraswatí. The nimble Brahmans worship the venerable Indra, to whom sweet liquids are offered, and to whom the melted butter is poured forth; therefore let materials for sacrifice be given us in abundance; both strength from drinking the moon-plant liquor, and more moon-plants to press.

20. O all-prospering moon-plant, when pressed, bring to us wealth accompanied with cows and horses; and let me obtain the white-coloured sweet juice, mingled with the produce of the cow. Do thou, O lord of all gold-coloured things, most brilliant Soma, when prepared by men, come for our glory, as a friend for friendship. Establish with us thy ancient friendship, banish from us every godless consuming (Rákshas). All-subduing Soma, destroy our opponents; root out the double-faced wretches.

21. The Brahmans adorn and adorn again, and adorn all around, and pacify the possessor of might,

and make him all-glorious with their sweet liquors, and those who purify him with their gold-ringed fingers, who moves in the watery regions aloft, and then drips down, and who amid the waters is the surveyor of all things. Sing to the intelligent purifying god, who rains down nourishment like a mighty shower, and who as a serpent casts its old skin, and who, capering like a horse, moves forward as the gold-coloured rainer of felicity. He who takes the lead, who shines in the waters, who is produced during the day, who is placed amid fluids, the gold-coloured god, bathed with pure water, the lovely-looking fluid, whose chariot is formed of rays of light, the possessor of all wealth, who has been domiciled by us, is now being purified.

[End of the sixteenth Adhyáya.]

SEVENTEENTH ADHYÁYA.

1. O Agni, son of strength, with all thy attendant fires accept of this our sacrifice and our song of praise, and give us food; for although we worship each of the other gods, it is into thee (that our offerings) are cast. O lord of all, the joyful, the celebrated divinity, exhibit thy love to us, that we, the friends of Agni, may love thee.

2. O my friends, we worship your Indra for the

benefit of all people. May he manifest himself only to us. O giver of all gifts, sender of rain, unlock the treasury of this (overhanging) cloud, and speak for us, since to thee no one dare reply. The rainer of felicity, like a venerable (bull approaching) the herd, approaches the tribes of men as their lord, and to whom no one dare reply.

3. Do thou, who takest up with us thy abode, and art worthy to be reverently approached, do thou send us wealth, with preservation; since, O Agni, thou art the conveyer of wealth into this world. Do thou also confer distinction on our sons. O Agni, do thou save our sons and grandsons with thy preserving, indestructible, united (aids). Remove far from us the wrath of the gods, and the murderous violence of men.

4. What, O Vishnu, is that most sacred name of thine which thou utterest when thou sayest "I am all-glorious?" Do not conceal thy radiant form from us, and be with us in thy other (guileful) form in the field of battle. O all-glorious lord, who art acquainted with all the subjects of knowledge, I now praise that name of thine. Mighty also (in thy cause), I celebrate thee who dwellest far distant from this terrestrial world. When, O Vishnu, I utter the word Vashat for thee, then do thou, as the all-glorious one, honour my oblation with acceptance. Let my well-sung hymns of

praise extol thee, and do you[1] always preserve me with all kinds of preservation.

5. O Váyu, I, rendered glorious by the performance of sacred rites, and desirous of heaven, come to thee the first[2] with the sweet moon-plant juice. O god, worthy of all regard, come to our moon-plant banquet, drawn by thy million of horses. O Indra and Váyu, ye are worthy to drink of that expressed moon-plant juice; for the streams of liquid flow together naturally unto you as waters into a pit. O Váyu and Indra, mighty, and the lords of might, do ye come to the moon-plant banquet for our protection in your chariot drawn by a million of horses.

6. On the recession of night, (Soma), prepared anew, advances for the production of nourishment, when the exertions of the preparers of the sacrifice set him in motion towards (the receiving-vessel). We bring forth pure that (essence) of his, the liquor drunk so abundantly by Indra, which the moving singers of sacred song, both formerly and at the present time, quaff with their mouths.[3] The priests praise the purifier in their primeval hymns, while,

---

1 The original here changes from the singular to the plural, according in this with the modern Indian languages.

2 The wind or air, naturally by evaporation, carries off the first share of the liquid.

3. *Or*, the divine cows eat the stalks with their mouths.

by bending, the supporting fingers are strengthened to raise up (the oblation) for the gods.

7. I prepare to propitiate, with hymns of adoration, Agni, lord paramount over sacrifices, and like a long-tailed horse.[1] May he who is the lord of strength, the great traveller, and possessed of beautiful features, be to us without fail the rainer of felicity. May he who goes every where save us at all times from sinful men, both far off and at hand.

8. O slayer of foes, thou subduest in the wars all our opponents; thou art the destroyer of the power of the Daitya, and producer (of that of the gods); thou art the destroyer of all our foes, and the annihilator of those who rise against us. O Indra, heaven and earth take refuge in thy strength as a child does in its mother; and when thou slayest thy all-encircling foe, every one of thy opponents becomes enfeebled at the contemplation of wrath.

9. The sacrifice makes Indra grow great, so that he manifests himself on the earth, making the clouds come over the heavens. Exhilarated by the moon-plant beverage, Indra enlarges the shining firmament and strikes through the mighty cloud. He brought back their cows to the sons of Angiras,

---

[1] *i. e.* sweepest away thy foes as such a horse the flies; *elsewhere* 'váravantam' is rendered a war-horse.

bringing them to light when they were concealed in the cave, and laid low Bala (the prince of the Pani).

10. Do ye extol Indra, who is the subduer of hosts, and ever encircled with songs of praise, and bring him here for our protection; him who subdues in war, but cannot be subdued or slain, the drinker of the moon-plant beverage, the bearer away of the sacrifice, whose prowess cannot be resisted. O Indra, throne of praise, and all-wise, give us riches in abundance; save us by the wealth of our foes.

11. Thy internal vigour [1] is great, thy prowess is all-powerful, and thy intellect sharpens thy illustrious Vajra. Heaven, O Indra, extols thy heroism, the earth publishes thy fame; thee the waters and mountains serve as their lord. The mighty, all-preserving Vishnu, and Mitra, and Varuna praise thee; thee also the powerful bands of Maruts delight.

12. O brilliant Agni, men utter the language of adoration to obtain strength. Destroy our foes by these (thy aids). O Agni, bring for us, desirous of cows, large stores of wealth; and do thou, the cause of abundance, abundantly supply us. Do not

---

[1] The turn the Bháshya gives to the word 'indriya' is coarse; I have expressed the sense.

cast us off in this war, as one casts off a burden, but bring into our possession the wealth that covers our enemies.

13. All the moving tribes of men bow down before the wrath of Indra, as all the rivers bend towards the sea. He strikes off the head of the earth-shaking Vritra with his rain-causing, hundred-spiked Vajra.[1] His might has been gloriously displayed, and Indra rolls up and spreads out both heaven and earth, as men do a skin-carpet.

14. Let thy intelligent, riches-conveying, pleasing, easy-going horses come to us. Do thou, of pleasing form, and causer of rain, approach thy splendid, chariot-drawing horses, (that convey to us) the object of our adoration. Receive blessings on your heads; for (Indra), who points to happiness with all his ten fingers, stands amid the sacrificial waters.

[End of the seventeenth Adhyáya.]

---

[1] Any one who has witnessed, from the top of some one of the lofty Indian mountains, a thunder-storm at a distance,—the thick black clouds covering the plains, the forked lightning darting from an electric cloud higher up in the heavens, and the torrents of rain that afterwards descended with the dissolution of the black clouds,—will be able to appreciate the poetry of Indra's battle with Vritrásur.

EIGHTEENTH ADHYÁYA.

1. Get ready in haste the moon-plant beverage, worthy of all praise, for the valiant hero (Indra), for his exhilaration. Let the two powerful horses, who partake of the sacrificial food, bring Indra to us, who acts like a friend, and is worshipped by sacred song. Let the quaffer of the moon-plant juice, the slayer of Vritra, come; and when he comes, let him never depart, but let him with his hundred auxiliaries restrain our foes.

2. Let the moon-plants enter thee, O Indra, as the rivers do the sea; for there is no one thing that surpasses thee. O rainer of felicity, all-wakeful Indra, thou in thy might didst manifest thyself to partake of the Soma juice, which diffuses itself through all thy abdomen. O slayer of Vritra, let the moon-plant juice be diffused abundantly throughout thy abdomen, and let the floods of shining liquor be diffused through the glorious bodies (of the gods).

3. O Agni, who art addressed in songs of praise, enter the sacred (place), for the benefit of every sacrificer, to prosper the sacred rites; for there the hymn is sung to Rudra,[1] which procures his pre-

---

[1] Rudra is here a name of Agni. There is no notice of Śiva in this Veda, unless he be through Rudra identified with Agni.

sence. May he, the mighty one, the unmeasured, known by his smoky ensign, all-joyous, satisfy us in respect of solemn rites and supplies of food. May that Agni, who is lord of all, the divine, who acts to us as a signal, and is possessed of great radiance, hear us when engaged in our sacred songs.

4. Do ye sing, while the sacrifice is going on to the much-invoked destroyer of foes, the song which delights the powerful god, as (grass does) the cow. The every-where-diffused Indra does not withhold the gift of food joined to cows, when he hears our songs of praise; for it was he, the slayer of foes, that entered the crowded cow-house of the host-destroying Paṅi, and by his mighty aids brought the cows to light.

5. This Vishnu, when he made his tour of the world, put down his foot but three times, and covered all (the earth) with the dusty (sole of his foot). Vishnu the preserver, the indefatigable, made the journey in three steps, and thus upheld the performance of sacred rites. Regard well the works of Vishnu; for on their account are you allowed to put your hand to sacred rites. He is the intimate companion and friend of Indra. The glorious sages look to the steps of Vishnu, as to the radiance spread through the heavens. The Brahmans, singers of eucharistic hymns, and ever-wakeful, glorify that

supreme footstep of Vishnu. Since Vishnu has made that journey over the seven regions of the earth, let the gods preserve us.[1]

6. Let not thy priests engage in their delightful services at a distance from us; and shouldst thou be at a distance, come to our joyous assembly, and, remaining in our presence, listen to our (songs of praise). These, the singers of thy sacred hymns, sit amid the vessels of moon-plant juice, as a fly does in a pot of honey; and the singers, desirous of wealth, rest for the object of their desire with confidence on Indra, as a man puts his foot on a chariot.

7. It is he that receives praise, therefore do ye chant the ancient solemn word of Brahmá, and sing the pristine long psalter adapted to the sacrifice, and procure intellectual endowments for our singer. Let Indra rain down on us abundance of wealth; let him give us land, and make us glorious as the Sun, since our white, pure libations of moon-plant juice, mingled with the produce of the cow, delight Indra.

8. O Soma, thou art poured out for Indra, the slayer of Vritra, for his drinking; for he is the giver of gifts, and the god who, like a heron, sits in the assembly of men. Do ye, O my learned

---

[1] This paragraph refers to the Vámana Avatár.

friends, along with us, both partake of and worship the all-brilliant, powerful, food-inhabiting (Soma). [*Pavityam harijantam—as before.*]

9. [*Kastamindra — as before.*] O possessor of riches, prosper in these wars those who bestow on thee delight-inspiring, sacrificial viands. O possessor of the horses Harí, through the songs with which we adore thee, may we with our sons escape from all our difficulties. O ye priests, do ye sprinkle (for Indra) the sweet juice of the sweet, nourishing (plant); for that heroic god, who always grows great on sacrifices, is the object of our praises.

10. O Indra, who ridest on the horses Harí, there is no one who now is able to do justice to thy praise, as it was celebrated of old, through deficiency in might and reverence. We, desirous of food, call upon your Indra, lord of provisions, who grows great by our sacrifices, performed by men not inattentive to their duties.

11. Do ye celebrate him, who carries the (sacrifice) to heaven; for the terrestrial gods approach their divine lord, and thou, Agni, forwardest the sacrifice into the midst of the gods. Do thou, our chanter, praise Agni, the all-liberal giver of wealth, who is manifested with varied radiance, and who is the primeval god, the receiver of this moon-plant oblation, that the sacrifice may be prosperous when all the rites are performed.

12. O Soma, when pressed by the stones, thou movest across the goat's-hair strainer, which thy green juice, proceeding from the boards, enters, and afterwards takest up thy abode in the waters, as a man does in a city. Soma, desirous of affording nourishment, is purified by moving across the sheep's-hair strainer, and appears like a high-spirited horse, rejoicing, and purified by the learned priests and sacred hymns.

13. We give the liquor to the holder of the thunderbolt to drink. Do thou bring the expressed juice for the oblation, and let him come to honour us with his presence, while listening to the sacred hymns. Himself a thief, he keeps off thieves, and, though a slayer of travellers, is reverentially worshipped in the highways. Honour, O Indra, with acceptance this (liquor) of ours, and this song, and come with all varied mental endowments.

14. O Indra and Agni, illuminators of heaven, ye two appear glorious in the wars; your might is there peculiarly conspicuous. [*Indragni—see before; Indráya—before; Ka—before.*[1]]

15. As an elephant in search (of a foe) drops a fragrant juice from his temples, so does (Indra)

---

[1] These texts having occurred before, in the MSS. only the beginning is given, and the Bháshya does not again explain them.

distil a liquid juice, the product of many libations. No one, O mighty god, can restrain thee; and when thou hast drunk the expressed moon-plant juice, thou movest every where by thy might; Indra, the mighty one, never to be overcome, always stable, arrayed in armour for the war, and the possessor of riches, and who, when he hears the invocation of the chanter, never recedes from us, but comes into his presence.

16. The clean, brilliant, purified vessels of moon-plant juice are being prepared while all the holy hymns are being recited. The purifying juice descends from heaven and from the mid-air, and is prepared on the earth, upon the elevated strainer. The all-diffusive, white, brilliant (streams of juice), which destroys all that hate us, are now being prepared.

17. I call on Indra and Agni, the beaters down of our foes, and destroyers of our enemies, the all-victorious and invincible, the bestowers of food. [*The next two lines were given before.*]

18. We, who are employed in providing sacrificial food, prepare in thy presence, O Agni, produced by might (of man), a pleasing, divine, introduction-procuring song. O Agni, whose appearance is that of burnished gold, we approach the place of thy shining presence as (a traveller seeks) the shade. He, the slayer of our foes, is like a

fierce warrior, or like a sharp-horned, quick-advancing bull. O Agni, it was thou that didst burn down the cities.[1]

19. We desire the presence of the faithful friend of all men, the preserver of the flame of the sacrifice, the indestructible, brilliant god. He who through sacrificial rites saves the world from all evils, became visible, and, bringing the world to acquiesce in our desires, created the different seasons. Agni, the desire of all that has received, and all that will receive existence, shines forth as supreme lord in all the worlds of delight.

[End of the eighteenth Adhyáya.]

NINETEENTH ADHYÁYA.

1. Agni, the performer of wondrous works, adorns his own person with the ancient hymn that is now to be produced, and grows great through the means of learned Brahmans. I call upon Agni, the descendant of food, possessed of pure radiance, to be

---

[1] Tripurásura had three cities; one of iron, one of silver, and one of gold. These, according to the common legend, were burnt down by Śiva. The commentator therefore adds, that the Śiva who burnt the cities was Rudra, and he, according to the Vedas, is Agni; or else Agni is said to have caused the conflagration, from Śiva having used a burning arrow. See third paragraph of this Adhyáya.

present in this indestructible sacrifice. O Agni, who with thy radiant flame art worthy of all honour from thy friends, sit down on the sacred grass.

2. O Soma, bruised by stones, thy might, which cleaves through the Rákshasas, here takes its station. Disperse all who fight against us. Thou, by thy might, art the destroyer of foes, so that I praise thee, and place the enemies' wealth in my chariot. The solemnities of thee, the purifier, cannot be broken in upon by the evil-minded Rákshasas. Do thou break to pieces those that fight against thee. The priest sends forward into the sacred waters the joy-distilling, might-conferring juice.

3. Come, O Indra, with thy peacock-feather-resembling horses. Let no caster of snares draw thee away from us, but come here with the celerity of one passing through the land of Dhanwa.[1] Indra is the devourer of Vritra, overthrower of Bala, destroyer of cities, shedder down of water, he who mounts his chariot when the two horses Harí neigh, and the carrier by assault of the enemies' strongholds. Thou feedest the institutor of the sacrifice, as a cow-herd does his cows, and as the cows lick

---

[1] Said in the Bháshya to be Márwár. It contains but little water; hence the need of expedition.

up the grass; and as streams flow into the lake, (so do the streams of liquor into thee).

4. As the red stag when thirsty goes to the lake, free of moss and weeds, so do thou come quickly to us, who have obtained thy friendship, and drink along with the sons of Kańwa. O Indra, possessor of riches, let the moon-plant juice delight thee, that thou mayest give wealth to the institutor of the moon-plant sacrifice. It was when thou didst covertly drink the Soma juice, poured into the ladle, that thou didst become possessed of thy primeval might.

5. O thou possessed of great might, thou, as an all-glorious divinity, art the object of human praise. O possessor of riches, thou art the bestower of happiness, therefore I address thee in hymns of praise; let not thy riches ever come to an end. O god, who assignest to us a place of abode, let not thy auxiliary (Maruts ever fail) us. O aider of men, to us the far-seeing sages measure out all kinds of wealth.

6. She, the kind bringer to light of beings, the mother (of active labours), the destroyer (of darkness), the daughter of heaven, (the Morn,) succeeding to her sister (Night), shines forth. Swift as a horse, the mother of the rays of light, the friend of sacrifices, the friend of the Aświni Kumáras, is the goddess Aurora. Truly thou art the

friend of the Aświni Kumáras, the mother of the rays of light, and hast dominion over wealth.

7. This newly manifested, beloved morn, the destroyer of darkness, (descends) from heaven. O sons of Aświni, I praise your might; even you, who are worthy of being reverently approached, whose mother is the sea, you, who by your intelligence gain riches, and who, through sacred rites, give us a fixed place of abode. While your chariot is moving along in the much-extolled firmament, our praises receive expression.

8. O Aurora, partaker of sacrificial food, bring us collected stores of wealth, by which we may obtain sons and grandsons. O possessor of cows and horses, diffuser of radiance, famed for thy gracious, faithful words, do thou, to-day, in this place, keep darkness at a distance from our wealth-procuring rites. O partaker of sacrificial food, yoke to-day thy glowing horses, and bring to us all happiness-conferring things.

9. O all-enveloping sons of Aświni, destroyers of foes, of subdued minds, give us valuable, pleasure-conferring wealth, so that we may obtain a livelihood: get now on your chariot, (and come) into our presence. O gods, dispellers of disease, destroyers of foes, possessed of the golden chariot, let your horses, which are ready in the morning, bring you here to the drinking of the moon-plant

beverage. Ye, after the instituted mode, produced the much-praised light in the heavens for the benefit of man; let the sons of Aświni bring for us strengthening food.

10. I praise Agni, the all-protecting home, to which the cows betake themselves for refuge, to which the fleet horses betake themselves, as well as the offerers of the daily sacrifices. O god, bring food for those who celebrate thy praise. The all-seeing Agni gives to the man (who worships him) a powerful (offspring). Agni, when propitiated, makes the riches flow in on us, which are produced in many places, and are productive of fame, and which may serve for gifts. O god, bring food, &c. O praise that Agni whom the cows approach, and the swift-going horses, and the noble-born sages. O god, bring, &c.

11. O brilliant Aurora, enlighten our minds as thou hast enlightened us in times past, that this day we may obtain much wealth. O thou of glorious origin, by whose aid we obtain horses, (favour me) Satyaśravas, son of Vayya. O recipient of praise, bringer of brilliant treasures, destroyer of darkness, daughter of heaven, powerful goddess, give us a place of abode. O thou, &c. May she to-day, who is the bringer of riches, the daughter of the Sun, the dispeller of darkness, the mighty goddess, to-day find us a place of abode. O thou, &c.

12. O sons of Aświni, the chanting Rishis adorn with hymns of praise thy most beloved, felicity-raining, wealth-conveying chariot. O ye skilled in all pleasure-conferring knowledge, do ye hear my invocation. O sons of Aświni, passing others, come to us, that I may always gain the advantage over all my foes. O piercers of the hearts of your foes, who ride in a golden chariot, bestowers of brilliant treasures, propellers of rivers, skilled in pleasure-conferring knowledge, hear my invocation. O sons of Aświni, come ye to us, bearing jewels, wearing the appearance of Rudras, having a golden chariot, possessors of the wealth of provisions, who are the objects of our worship, skilled, &c.

13. Agni is admonished by the fuel of the sacrificers, when the morning comes, in the same manner as is the cow; and the flames, bursting upwards, advance towards their (heavenly) seat, with the noise of mighty bulls amid the branches (of the trees of the forest). This sacrifice-forwarding Agni, when admonished to offer sacrifices to the gods, with kindly disposition rises aloft, and the might of the blazing, shining divinity, and the mighty god himself, delivers the world from darkness. When he looses the (dark) fetters of the (world's) tribes, the radiant Agni shines forth with brilliant rays. Afterwards, the prospering streams, flowing from the elevated strainer, come in contact with the

vessel, and, desiring to furnish nourishment, are drunk by Agni from the ladles.

14. This most excellent of lights comes, the all-glorious and all-revealing comes into being, diffusing himself abroad: and as Night is the daughter of the Sun, so does she direct her mind to the womb (of the Morn), for the production of the Dawn. The brilliant shining (Morn), foster-child of the radiant Sun, comes forth, and the dark (Night) fixes her mind on her neighbour's abode. They are a nearly related pair, immortal, mutually succeeding each other, and destroying one another in their passage through earth. The infinite paths of the sisters is one: instructed by the god (of day), it is traversed by them alternately. The creative Night and Morn are of one mind, but diverse in form, and neither encroach on each other, nor ever stand still.

15. Agni before the dawn shines forth; for the voices of the Brahmans, lovers of the gods, have raised themselves. O sons of Aświni, who go before our foes, who ride in chariots, do ye come to the splendid (sacrifice), complete in all its parts. O sons of Aświni, when you, first-rate travellers, most eagerly come in at the end of the well-prepared (sacrifice), do not reject it; for ye are here at present the objects of our praise. When the day commences do ye most eagerly come with your life-

preserving (viands) to the viandless sacrifice, bringing happiness to the master of the ceremonies. O come ye at the milking of the cows, at the dawn of day, at mid-day, and when the sun declines, night and day, with your felicitous preservation. Even now, O sons of Aświni, the banquet cannot proceed without you.

16. These intelligence-giving rays of morn spread light over the eastern aerial region; and the moving, creative, generative, morning rays, march forth like strong men arrayed in armour. The resplendent rays proceed forward with freedom, and, self-yoked, the glowing beams unite themselves (to the chariot). All intelligences awake with the morning, and the before-mentioned rays of the brilliant (goddess) pay their respects to the radiant Sun. The sacrifice-receiving Aurora is worshipped by one effort, even from afar,[1] and brings food without fail to the pious bountiful master of the moon-plant banquet.

17. The terrestrial fire is lightened up, the radiant Sun rises. The magnificent joyful Aurora encompasses all things with her radiance. Therefore let the sons of Aświni yoke their chariot to go to the banquet, and let the generative Sun bring into action all the various operations of the world. O sons of Aświni, when you yoke your rain-con-

---

[1] *i. e.* without the necessity of turning round.

veying chariot, distil to us strength along with the sweet water. Send us the food which is in (the enemies') camp, and grant that we may obtain wealth in the conflict of heroes. O sons of Aświni, let your three-wheeled, easy-going, swift-horsed, much-praised, triple-poled,[1] riches-bearing, all-resplendent chariot bring happiness into our presence, for the sake both of our bipeds and quadrupeds.

18. Let thy separated drops bring into our presence food in quantity manifold, like the drops of rain that fall from heaven. The gold-coloured divinity, who overlooks all the delight-inspiring hymns, distils the vapour that drives away the Rákshasas. The producer of virtuous actions, when purified by mortals, like a fearless king, sits after the manner of a hawk over the sacred waters. Thou, O Soma, when purified by dwelling in heaven, art manifested on earth. Do thou bring us all we wish.

[End of the nineteenth Adhyáya.]

TWENTIETH ADHYÁYA.

1. The streams of the distilling, expressed, divinity-pleasing juice pour out might to us. The creative singers and performers of sacred rites

---

[1] *i. e.* a pole composed of three pieces of wood, as is usual to this day in India.

purify the swift-moving, shining, increasing, extolled (moon-plant juice). O possessor of much wealth, fill up the extolled receiving-vessel with these glorious emanations from thy purified self.

2. I praise that Indra who is famed among the gods, who is the increaser of all, and manifested in every season. O lord of might, our no common songs seek access to thee.

[*Viśruta—see before.*]

3. [*Átvárатham—as before.*] O possessor of great might, performer of meritorious acts, worthy of divine worship, thou manifestest thyself with thy all-pervading might. With the might of thy mighty self, let thy two hands grasp the golden, earth-enveloping thunderbolt.

4. He who knows all ancient things, and when he comes to the ground where is the sacrificial assembly, blazes forth like a refreshing breeze, springing up in the heavens, and existing in his hundred forms, gives forth a radiance like that of the Sun. He who has a double birth, who flames forth from three places, enlightening all moving beings, who is the inviter of the gods, the principal offerer of oblations, takes his seat on the abode of the waters.[1] He who gives to him who is the in-

---

[1] The double birth is from two pieces of wood; *or*, by friction united with consecration; *or*, from heaven and earth. The three places are the three sacred fire-places.

viter of the gods, has a double birth, and holds all valuable things for the purpose of giving them in exchange for sacrificial food, will obtain a virtuous son.

5. O Agni, to-day we extol thee with floods of songs, who (bearest away our sacrifices) like a horse, art to us a kind benefactor, and desired by us with all our hearts. In very truth, O rite-prospering Agni, thou hast become the conveyer of this prosperous, propitious, desire-fulfilling, properly-conducted mingled oblation. O Agni, shining as the Sun, propitious, and surrounded with all thy radiance, come into our presence with all those heavenly essences.

6. O immortal Agni, who knowest the place of all beings, bring to us from the regions of the morning, for the matter of the sacrifice, wealth which procures an excellent place of abode, and convey to us the gods that love to come in the morning. Thou, O Agni, art the object of our rites, the herald of the gods, the conveyer of the offering, the chariot to bring the gods to the sacrifice, along with the Aświni Kumáras and the goddess Aurora. Grant us bodily vigour and abundance of food.

7. The weakling reduces to nothing the warrior and the destroyer in battle of many cities, even although in the prime of life. Behold the ingenuity

and might of this god; to-day he dies, to-morrow he revives. He is mighty through his might, red in his appearance, possessed of beauteous wings; he is powerful, eternal, and without a fixed abode. He unfailingly accomplishes all that he conceives, lets nothing prove vain, but obtains by conquest, which he freely bestows. In union with the Maruts, the holder of the thunderbolt, the slaughterer of Vritra, sends down showers. These gods set themselves to the work of producing water in the mighty firmament, by the mighty means required for the beloved art.

8. This moon-plant juice has been expressed; therefore let the Maruts, who shine with unborrowed radiance, and the sons of Aświni, drink of it. Mitra, and Aryamá, and Varuna also drink of the newly-produced juice, purified by the strainer, and occupying three places.[1] Indra, in an especial manner, expresses his delight like a chanter, honouring with acceptance, early in the morning, this expressed juice mixed with the produce of the cow.

9. Truly, O Súrya, thou art mighty. Truly, O Áditya,[2] thou art mighty; and the might of thee, the mighty (god), is above all praise. O glorious divinity, thou art mighty through thy inherent

[1] *i. e.* the strainer, receiving-vessel, and oblation-receiving fire-place.

[2] This and Súrya are names of the Sun.

might. Truly thou art mighty, O Súrya, through thy fame. Thou art, indeed, mighty, O brilliant god. Thou, by thy might, art the destroyer of Asurs, and the instructor of the gods, whose radiance is all-expansive and indestructible.

10. O lord of inebriating liquors, come into our presence with thy two horses Harí, to the banquet of expressed juice; come into our presence with thy horses Harí. O Indra, slayer of Vritra, and performer of meritorious acts, well acquainted with these two differing modes of action, come, &c. Thou art viewed as the slayer of Vritra, and thou art the drinker of the moon-plant liquor. Come, &c.

11. Do ye, for the obtaining of much wealth, bring the oblation forward for the mighty (Indra), and raise a joyful song of praise to obtain greater intelligence. (O Indra), satisfier of men, run to the men who satisfy thee (with oblations). O ye Brahmans, do ye prepare a well-sung hymn of praise and sacrificial viands to the mighty Indra, who occupies an immeasurably extended space. The gods, possessors of intelligence, will never injure his rites.

12. The voices of the singers rise around (Indra), whose rage no one can withstand, who is lord of all, in order that he may subdue our foes. Do ye extol our brother possessor of the two horses Harí. I am lord of whatever Indra possesses; therefore, O

giver of wealth, I can support the chanter of the praises of the gods, nor will I ever consign him to poverty. (When Indra says) "I bestow wealth on him who day by day performs my worship, wherever he may be," (the Brahman replies) "O possessor of riches, there is no one else who bestows gifts like thee, none worthy of equal praise, no one else who cherishes us as a father."

13. Hear the call of the bruising-stone of me, the quaffer of the moon-plant beverage; attend to the song of the worshipping Brahman, and make these present services of mine productive of prosperity. Knowing the power of him who slew the Asurs, I never abandon the celebration of the praise of him who slew them, nor cease to proclaim his renown. On the contrary, O thou possessor of self-acquired celebrity, I ever publish thy fame. O possessor of riches, thy moon-plant banquets are many among men, and many are the hymns of praise that are sung to thee; therefore do not linger in coming, or ever remove to a great distance from us.

14. Praise ye the might of that Indra who sits in the front of the chariot, who makes us stand firm in battle, even in the close conflict, who is the slayer of clouds of foes[1] and the sender (of riches):

---

[1] This phrase is a translation of Vritra.

let him attend to our (solemn songs), and cause that the relaxed strings of our enemies' bows be broken in pieces. Thou createst the down-flowing flood, thou strikest through the all-enveloping cloud.[1] Thou art without a foe, the preserver of every valuable thing. We embrace thee; therefore do thou cause, &c. Let all the far-seeing minds of our foes suffer destruction; and, O Indra, cast thy slaughtering weapon amid the enemies who wish to slay us, and be to us a bestower of wealth by conferring (on us their spoil); and do thou cause, &c.

15. Let the praises of a rich, wealthy, famous god like thee, who art served by the horses Harí, be especially blessed with wealth; and let the hater of those who apply not themselves to sacred music accept our well-chanted psalter and well-sung hymns of praise. O Indra, never deliver us over to the murderous crew, never permit us to be conquered, but by thy acts, O mighty god, teach us (to vanquish).

16. Come, O Indra, to the eucharistic hymns of Kańwa with thy horses Harí; and whilst thou rulest over the firmament, do thou, uniting with the shining offering, go thy way to heaven. In this sacrifice (Soma), the axle of these (bruising-stones), makes (the stalks) to shake as a wolf does a flock of sheep.

---

[1] This phrase is also a translation of Vritra.

Whilst thou rulest, &c. Let the moon-plant bruising-stone, making a noise, bring thee, (O Soma,) to us by its voice. Whilst thou rulest, &c.

17. O most pleasant exhilarating Soma, flow out pure for Indra. Thy pressed, wisdom-giving white streams send forth their sound. The men who are as ready for food, as a waggon is for its load, prepare (the juice) for the banquet of the gods.

18. I praise Agni, the inviter to the sacrifice, the giver of gifts, the giver of a place of abode, the son of strength, the knower of all things, who carries aloft the offering with his all-collecting power, and embraces the white, flaming, brilliant, flowing stream of offered up melted butter. O most intelligent god, we, the institutors of sacrifices, offer up oblations to him who is most worthy of offerings, the eldest descendant of Angiras, beloved when attended by the wise priests, and resplendent when served with sacred hymns, going every where like the Sun, the inviter of the gods for the benefit of man, the white-haired, the rainer of felicity, thee our people especially propitiate that thou mayest send (them to heaven). He also, by his shining powerful might blazing forth, slays those that hate us, slays our haters, as with a battle-axe. By meeting with whom also the firm impenetrable fortress is swept away as if it were but a stream of water; who, pressing

on, subdues his foes, and never recedes, just as brave archers never draw back.

[End of the twentieth Adhyáya.]

TWENTY-FIRST ADHYÁYA.

1. O Agni, possessor of resplendent treasures, thy stores of food are renowned, thy radiance is of exceeding brilliance. O sage, possessor of glorious rays, it is thou that bestowest on the institutors of sacrifice food worthy of being commemorated. O possessor of purifying radiance, of shining radiance, and of abiding radiance, do thou come to us with thy luminous beams. And as a son coming to light from thy mother wood, save us and preserve the two worlds. O descendant of food, who knowest all beings,[1] rejoice in our hymns of praise, and be satisfied with our works. The multiform, wonderously-protecting sacrificial viands are being offered up to thee. Thou, O immortal Agni, encountering our earth-born foes, bestowest on us abundant wealth; and thyself of a form pleasant to approach, thou shinest forth and fillest up to us the reward of our acceptable rites. (We praise thee), the performer of sacrifice,

---

[1] Translation of 'Játavedas,' which is elsewhere translated 'possessor of wealth,' and 'possessor of knowledge.'

the all-wise, the possessor of great wealth, the giver of renowned gifts. It is thou, the possessor of riches, that bestowest stores of provisions and wealth worthy of acceptance. Men having placed thee, the true, the worshipful, the reverently-to-be-approached Agni, in thy recess to procure happiness, (other) men in pairs (extol) with their voices thee, the acute-eared, all-expanded associate of the gods.

2. O Agni, by thy aids (the sacrificer), that is to say, he to whom thou affordest the benefit of thy friendship, when supplied with brave heroes, and food, and sacred rites, overcomes all. O recipient of divine service, the watery, cart-conveyed, spring-produced, shining god is offered up to thee Thou, on account of thy power, art beloved by the morn, for thou shinest forth from amid the encircling gloom of night.

3. The vegetable tribes lay hold on Agni, when lying in the womb of the seasons, and the maternal waters bring him forth. Again, in like manner, at all times the trees and shrubs give him birth.

4. Agni pours forth his offering for Indra, and with his white radiance shines in the firmament, and, like a she-buffalo, produces abundance (for the gods).

5. Him who is the ever-wakeful the sacred hymns delight. Him who is the ever-wakeful the holy songs encircle. To him who is the ever-wakeful

the moon-plant liquor says, (Lay hold of me,) for to obtain thy friendship I am stationed here.

6. Agni, who is ever-wakeful, the sacred hymns delight; [*and so on, as the last.*]

7. We prostrate ourselves before the friendly divinities, who have previous to the sacrifice taken their seat; we prostrate ourselves before the gods, who are seated altogether. I now apply myself to the song which has a hundred measures and proceeds in a hundred paths. I apply myself to the song which proceeds in a hundred paths. I sing the thousand-direction-taking Sáma, composed in the Gáyatri, Trishtup, and Jagati metres. The Sáma, composed in the Gáyatri, Trishtup, and Jagati metres, the singers hold up in all its parts, and the gods there take up their abode.

8. Agni is radiance, and Radiance is Agni; Indra is radiance, and Radiance is Indra. The Sun is radiance, and Radiance is the Sun. O Agni, again and again supply us with strength, with food, and with long life; again and again save us from our sins. O Agni, supply us with wealth, water us on all sides with free, enjoyment-affording streams.

9. When I, O Indra, shall become a possessor of wealth like thee, then assuredly my singer of sacred hymns shall possess abundance of cows. When, O all-powerful god, I shall become a lord of cows, then shall I bestow the wealth I wish to give to

this singer of sacred song. My pleasant voice is the nourishing milch-cow which milks out cows and horses for the institutor of this moon-plant sacrifice.

10. O ye Waters, be to us promoters of happiness, and stand on our side to procure for us provisions and highly felicitous foresight. Let your most prospering juices be ministered to us in this world with the readiness that affectionate mothers (supply their infants). We cast you on (our bodies) with celerity, you who delight us by the destruction of our sins.[1] Ye Waters, also procure for us an (illustrious) progeny.

11. O Wind, let thy soothing delicious medicine enter our breasts, and do thou greatly extend our term of life. O Wind, thou art to us even as a father, even as a brother, to us even as an intimate friend. Do thou work with us for the preservation of the life-preserving sacrifice. O Wind, bestow on us, to afford us a living, a portion of that unfailing (wealth) which is in thy house carefully stored up.

12. The fiery divinity, gracefully spreading his wings, powerful and multiform, supporting his gold-coloured, flame-enveloped, feeding wood, and clothing himself time by time with the solar radiance,[2]

---

[1] *Or*, we reverently approach you who make our habitation comfortable.

[2] The Śruti thus explains this allusion. The Sun, at the time

and in his own proper person, manifests himself in every sacrifice. The seminal, multiform radiance is the sustainer of fluids, the same is the supporter of the dry ground; and spreading his glory through the heavens, he calls for the essence of Soma, the rainer of felicity. He, surrounded with his thousand flames, worthy of a share in the sacrifice, lays hold on the solar radiance. He, the giver of thousands, the giver of hundreds, the giver of manifold gifts, is the sustainer of heaven and the protector of the inhabitants of earth.

13. O Garuda, the men whose breasts are filled with devotional feeling see thee while moving thy wings gracefully in the heavens, as thou art radiant like gold, and the messenger of Varuna, art the bird that producest in the womb of Yama the all-controlling (Agni), and art the nourisher (of men). The water-preserving, aloft-going Garuda takes his station before us in the heavens, lays hold of his variegated armour, and coming himself with his own glorious plumage, like the Sun, to await our reverential view, he gives birth to the adorable, beloved (showers of rain). Covered with watery drops in the heavens, and shining with the light of the water-collecting (Sun), he goes to the fluid-

---

of his setting, enters Agni; and on this account fire appears brilliant at a much greater distance during the night than during the day.

receiving (cloud); and the Sun, shining with his white radiance, produces through the three worlds the delightful (rain).[1]

[End of the twenty-first Adhyáya.]

TWENTY-SECOND ADHYÁYA.

1. The fleet Soma, who is terrible as a sharp-horned bull, who slays his foes and vexes their men, who controls all living creatures, and never shuts his eyes, though himself but a single hero, subdues by one effort a hundred hosts. O warriors, ye obtain the victory by means of the life-controlling, conquering, warring, immoveable, all-supporting Indra, who never shuts his eyes, and subdues your foes by his arrow-holding, rain-dispensing hand. This Indra is armed with darts in his hands, and with drawn swords: with his band he engages in close conflict in the battle, conquers in close conflict, drinks the moon-plant beverage, has powerful arms, has his bow drawn, and slays his foes with his arrows shot abroad.

2. O Vrihaspati, surround us with thy chariot, for thou art the slayer of the Rákshasas, the destroyer of foes, the breaker of armies, the slaughterer in

---

[1] Garuda is the well-known vehicle of Vishnu, and, properly speaking, is a deified eagle.

war, the causer of victory, the preserver of our chariots. O Indra, do thou, who knowest the seat of water, hast experience of all might, and art possessed of stable heroism and surpassing bravery, all-powerful, fleet, the subjugator, the terrible god, who subduest heroes, subduest all beings, art the producer of might, stand up on thy conquering chariot. O my friends, who are the companions of my youth, do ye in alternate bands ascribe heroism to Indra, and call upon him, who is the clearer of water,—bringing clouds, and who knows where water is, who has in his hand the thunderbolt, who is victorious in war, and stays his foes by his might.

3. Let Indra, who pierces the watery cloud by his might, the ruthless hero, who is terrible in his wrath, that cannot be moved from his place, the subduer of armies, invincible in war, preserve our armies in the battle. Let Indra, the leader of the gods, and Vrihaspati, and Soma, the prosperer of sacrifices, march in front; and let the Maruts also advance at the head of the foe-subduing, conquering army of the gods. Let the mighty strength of the rain-dispensing Indra, of the radiant Varuna, and of the Maruts, descended from the mother of the gods, (be manifested.) Now the shout of victory rises from the mighty, earth-shaking, victorious gods.

4. O possessor of riches, render sharp our weapons, rejoice the minds of our foot-soldiers. O slayer of Vritra, let the triumphant shout of our fleet horsemen and triumphant chariots rise aloft. (Be with) our people, O Indra, when they come up to the standards of the enemy, and let our arrows gain the victory: let our heroes be superior, and let the gods be our preservers in the battle. O Maruts, envelope that hostile army of enemies, contending against us, in such activity-paralyzing darkness that one man shall not know another.

5. O Sin-maintaining goddess,[1] do thou remove far (from us), and, infatuating their minds, seize the limbs (of our foes); and, coming up to them, utterly consume their hearts with grief, and let murky darkness gather around our foes. O heroes, go forward and conquer, and may Indra confer on you felicity; let your arm be firm and invincible, as you yourselves are; having prepared your incantation-whetted, foe-destroying (arrows), cast them on the enemy; advance with a quick pace upon the foe, and leave not a whit of them.

6. Let the swift-flying herons, O Indra, come to them; let their army become a feast to the kite. Save none of them, (not even the pious;) as to the sinner, he cannot be saved: let the birds gather

---

[1] This is a kind of personification of Sin.

around and prey on the whole of them. O possessor of riches, let the enemy's army be surrounded with opponents, and do ye two, Indra and Agni, entirely consume it: where fall the arrows like boys without a *queue*, there let Brahmańaspati and Áditya give us prosperity, always grant us prosperity.

7. O slayer of Vritra, slay the Rákshasas and all that fight against us, burn up the foes that encircle us, consume the wrath of the enemies that would destroy us. Slay those that fight against us, and bring down those who wish to gather an army against us. Do ye seek when the contest takes place for your aid, first Indra's two arms, which are large, youthful, incapable of being restrained, strong as the world-supporting elephant, and indomitable; for by them the might of the Asurs was subdued.

8. I cover over all my vital parts with a coat of mail. O Soma, do thou sprinkle me over with Amrita. O Varuna, let the gods make thee the possessor of great felicity, and delight thee, the victorious divinity. May our enemies become blind as a headless snake, and let Indra slay all the chiefs of those who had been consumed by Agni. May all the gods slay the hateful foe that takes up a distant position and desires to murder us, and let the holy verse be my interposing coat of mail.

9. O Indra, terrible as a lion, who leaves the

dread-inspiring prints of his feet on the mountains on which he treads, do thou come to us even from the most distant regions. Having sharpened thy darting, sharp Vajra, destroy our enemies, and put to flight those that fight against us. Grant, O ye gods, that receive sacrifice, that we may hear only what is auspicious with our ears, and see only what is auspicious with our eyes; and may we who propitiate the gods arrive at the age laid down by the divinity with undiminished mental and bodily vigour.[1] May Indra, served with many sacrificial viands, grant us prosperity. May the nourishing Sun, who knows all things, grant us prosperity. May Tárkshya Rishi, the ring of whose chariot-wheel could not be cut, grant us prosperity. [O Triune divinity![2]] May Vrihaspati grant us prosperity. [Triune divinity! grant us prosperity.]

---

[1] The Bháshya says that some authorities make this age a hundred and sixteen, and others a hundred and twenty years.

[2] So I translate OM, as the Brahmans say it is intended to represent the one spirit, Brahm, who is manifested in Brahmá, Vishnu, and Śiva, and is composed of A, U, M, their symbols. This word, however, I am satisfied is a modern addition.

THE END.